Teaching Middle School Physical Education

This resource supports Middle School Physical Education teachers in promoting healthy activity levels among their students, both in and outside the PE facilities. Its comprehensive curricular approach addresses National Physical Education standards but, unlike traditional curricula, encourages teaching sports and fitness as connected components instead of separate. This book is rooted in the progressive Sport Education model, which facilitates students' personal growth with the learning of individual and team sports. Fitness programming and cooperative activities are key aspects of this program. Unique to this book is a section detailing what to do if students have not yet learned movement concepts and skills at the elementary level. Each chapter includes a list of key concepts and review questions. A rationale for the Sport Education model, lesson plans, sample assessments, and safety considerations are provided. Sample forms and documents round out the book for a seamless transition from elementary PE to the middle level. Middle School Physical Education teachers and PE administrators will find this classroom-tested curricular approach accessible and easy to implement. As your students undergo psychomotor, cognitive, and affective change throughout the middle-grade years, this book lays out a PE program that not only acknowledges, but celebrates, their development, and improves physical skills while working past any fitness weaknesses.

Michael E. Gosset is a Lecturer and Unit Coordinator for Physical Education for Hostos Community College (CUNY), USA.

Other Eye On Education Books Available from Routledge

(www.routledge.com/eyeoneducation)

Mathematics Teaching on Target: A Guide to Teaching for Robust Understanding at All Grade Levels
Studies in Mathematical Thinking and Learning Series
Alan Schoenfeld, Heather Fink, Alyssa Sayavedra,
Anna Weltman, Sandra Zuñiga-Ruiz

Place-Based Scientific Inquiry: A Practical Handbook for Teaching Outside
Benjamin Wong Blonder, Ja'Nya Banks, Austin Cruz,
Anna Dornhaus, R. Keating Godfrey, Joshua S. Hoskinson,
Rebecca Lipson, Pacifica Sommers, Christy Stewart,
Alan Strauss

Learning Through Movement in the K-6 Classroom: Integrating Theater and Dance to Achieve Educational Equity
Kelly Mancini Becker

Exploring Math with Technology: Practices for Secondary Math Teachers
Allison W. McCulloch, Jennifer N. Lovett

Introducing Nonroutine Math Problems to Secondary Learners: 60+ Engaging Examples and Strategies to Improve Higher-Order Problem-Solving Skills
Robert London

Integrating Racial Justice Into Your High-School Biology Classroom: Using Evolution to Understand Diversity
David Upegui, David E. Fastovsky

Reaching and Teaching Neurodivergent Learners in STEMStrategies for Embracing Uniquely Talented Problem Solvers
Jodi Asbell-Clarke

Teaching Middle School Physical Education

A Progressive Curricular Approach

Michael E. Gosset

NEW YORK AND LONDON

Designed cover image: © Getty Images

First published 2025
by Routledge
605 Third Avenue, New York, NY 10158

and by Routledge
4 Park Square, Milton Park, Abingdon, Oxon, OX14 4RN

Routledge is an imprint of the Taylor & Francis Group, an informa business

© 2025 Michael E. Gosset

The right of Michael E. Gosset to be identified as author of this work has been asserted in accordance with sections 77 and 78 of the Copyright, Designs and Patents Act 1988.

All rights reserved. No part of this book may be reprinted or reproduced or utilised in any form or by any electronic, mechanical, or other means, now known or hereafter invented, including photocopying and recording, or in any information storage or retrieval system, without permission in writing from the publishers.

Trademark notice: Product or corporate names may be trademarks or registered trademarks, and are used only for identification and explanation without intent to infringe.

ISBN: 9781032729534 (hbk)
ISBN: 9781032698366 (pbk)
ISBN: 9781003423201 (ebk)

DOI: 10.4324/9781003423201

Typeset in Palatino
by codeMantra

Access the Support Material: www.routledge.com/9781032698366

Sometimes in your life, you're fortunate to come across special human beings. The dedication for this book goes to an individual who has been extraordinarily influential in my recent professional career. Dr. Jacqueline DiSanto has been my colleague for over a decade. She has understood my goals in higher education, and has supported me throughout. With a remarkable grasp for intuition and the workplace, she continues to mentor me in the higher education realm. I thank her for her collegiality, friendship, and support.

Online Supplemental Resources

Some of the resources in this book can be accessed online by visiting this book's product page on our website: www.routledge.com/9781032698366 (then follow the links indicating support material, which you can then download directly).

- ◆ Understanding Softball Workbook
- ◆ Understanding Basketball Workbook

Contents

Introduction 1

1 **A Review of Movement Education and Skill Themes:
   What Does It Have to Do with Middle School Physical
   Education?** 5

   Movement Education 6
   Skill Themes 10
   Lesson Plans for Movement Education 17
   Lesson Plans for Skill Themes 22
   Chapter 1 Review 29
   Reading Comprehension Questions 29

2 **The Sport Education Model...and How to
   Progress to It from Chapter 1** 31

   Why Did We Need Chapter 1? What Does it Have
   to Do with Middle School Physical Education? 31
   How Much Movement Education and Skill Themes
   Should Be Taught? Preparing for the Transition
   to Sport Education 32
   Sport Education Defined and Explained 36
   Understanding Volleyball 38
   Captains, Teams, and the Captain's Packet 52
   Volleyball Set 54
   The Season 55
   Volleyball 56
   Physical Education 63
   Player Roles 65
   Skill/Knowledge Checklist 66
   Game Preparation Criteria 66

viii ◆ Contents

Chapter 2 Review..67
Reading Comprehension Questions 68

3 Fitness..70
Components of Health-Related Fitness...................70
Rationale for Including Fitness in the Program 72
Integrating Fitness into a Lesson.............................73
Use as Part of Grading 76
Sharing with Parents 77
Fitness Report..78
Chapter 3 Review...79
Reading Comprehension Questions 79

4 Cooperative Activities 81
Why Cooperative Activities 81
Implementing Cooperative Activities.......................82
Chapter 4 Review...87
Reading Comprehension Questions 87

5 Assessment and Grading 88
How Do We Assess and Grade in Middle School? 88
The Domains of Learning..89
Assigning Percentages of Grading to Each Domain.............89
Chapter 5 Review...94
Reading Comprehension Questions 94

6 Intramurals..96
Team Selection..97
Scheduling of Intramurals..101
Scoring of Intramurals 103
Intramural Sports Rules..103
Chapter 6 Review...108
Reading Comprehension Questions 108

7 Summary and Student Success Stories 109

Index 113

Introduction

You are a middle school physical education teacher, or are about to begin as one! Depending on the way your school district is structured or organized, you may or may not know what type of physical education program your youngest, incoming students had in elementary school. Another possibility is that these students may have come from outside your district. This book was written to offer you an integrated approach to teaching physical education that was highly successful for my students, as well as myself, and many others over the years. I say that based on my enjoyment, my students' learning based on assessments, and student enjoyment based on their comments over the years.

Middle school is a time period of many changes for children. Understanding and responding to the developmental characteristics of 10- to 15-year-olds in culturally responsive and fulfilling ways is central to educating middle school children (Bishop & Harrison, 2021). During early adolescence, a period of growth and development between childhood and adolescence, children experience rapid development, form beliefs and attitudes, and acquire health habits and social behaviors that form the base for adulthood (McCarthy et al., 2016). Though children this age share common developmental characteristics, each has unique perspectives and experiences (Mertens & Caskey, 2018).

In other words, they are physically, cognitively, and emotionally changing. These are the "domains" of learning (psychomotor, cognitive, and affective, respectively), and physical education is the only subject area in the school to work consistently with all three of them. **Physically**, they are changing and growing, and that was a reason for writing my first book (*Lesson Plans for the Elementary PE Teacher: A Developmental Movement Education and Skill Themes Framework*). I had found from my research (Gosset, 2019) that more upper elementary students had a better attitude toward Physical Education in classes taught using the skill themes approach than those in classes taught using the multi-activity approach. That is, children may *know* how to physically execute a skill, but may not be able to do so as their bodies have not "kept pace" with their cognitive, or knowledge, growth. To put in another way, some children's coordination may be lagging if they haven't grown yet. Also bear in mind that, on average, the female body grows 2 years earlier than the male body.

Cognitively, middle school students continue to be like sponges, being able to absorb concepts and information, as well as beginning to use higher other thinking skills (HOTS). Their brains are growing fast and changing rapidly (Ginsburg, 2022). **Emotionally**, hormones start, or continue, to take a front seat. Middle school students can be challenging, but some of my best years were when teaching these students. A challenge can be seen in their attitudes. Unfortunately, studies have suggested that middle school students' attitude toward physical education decreases throughout their years (Subramaniam and Silverman, 2007).

That was the impetus for the writing of this book...to provide a curriculum, and an approach or model to teaching it, which is both enjoyable and interesting to the students (as well as yourself), and accountable to your administration and parents. Most books for middle school physical education address content traditionally, by creating sport units that are typically seasonal (and corresponding to scholastic sports), along with fitness and assessment components. This book will address sports a different way, by using the Sport Education model. If you are not familiar with it, be ready for a good read, and its exciting implementation.

Most of us integrate fitness into our programs. In this book, fitness will be a part of each lesson. You will be shown how to hold children accountable for enjoying their strengths and working on their fitness weaknesses, which also can be reported, as well as explained to, parents. In order to have accountability, you must have assessment. You will be shown objective ways to assess all parts (read: all domains) of the physical education program.

Again, since you may or may not know what type of physical education program your youngest, incoming students received from elementary school, Chapter 1 provides a brief overview of what movement education is and why it is important for the youngest grades. Teaching (sport skills) by use of the skill themes approach (Graham, Holt-Hale, McEwen, & Parker, 1980) for upper elementary grades is also reviewed, along with a few lessons for both movement education and skill themes.

Chapter 2, then, discusses the transition from the skill themes approach into sports skills. What you may most benefit from is this special section on how to integrate movement education and skill themes into the first several lessons of your youngest middle school grade level classes. This is a way of ensuring that these students have at least somewhat of a movement vocabulary and sport skill background, and it is here where the theory of concept transfer is discussed. Chapter 2 next presents the Sport Education model, and how to further students' sport skills in a larger team environment. Dr. Siedentop brought Sport Education to the United States around 1994 to create what he called "authentic" sport experiences in school. I will provide a thorough explanation of what it is, and how it can be used with middle school students, along with a few lesson plans.

In Chapter 3 you will be introduced to how to incorp orate fitness/fitness education into the curriculum. The four health-related fitness components will be reviewed, along with why we should do so, how to assess fitness, and how to use it as part of your overall grading system. Students take "ownership" of it. You might find that this system is more comprehensive than you are accustomed to.

Chapter 4 will cover cooperative games and activities. In this age of socio-emotional learning, it remains quite important to work with others in solving problems. Problem-solving is a characteristic that employers look for in employees. As is with all other areas in this book, it will involve progressions from pairs to small groups to large groups.

Chapter 5 is assessment and grading. As mentioned above, physical education uses all three domains, and thus is assessed in all three of them. This may be a controversial area, but it allows for accountability throughout the program. You will find assessment ideas, forms/templates, and rubrics.

Finally, Chapter 6 deals with Intramurals. Intramurals are sport competitions among students in school, but outside of class. You will see how teams are selected in a fair manner.

References

Teaching middle school physical education: A progressive curricular approach uses progressions in all areas.

Bishop, P., & Harrison, L. (2021). The evolving middle school concept. *Current Issues in Middle Level Education. 25*(2). https://files.eric.ed.gov/fulltext/EJ1288122.pdf

Ginsburg, C. (2022). https://parentandteen.com/adolescent-brain-development/

Gosset, M. (2019). *Lesson plans for the elementary PE teacher: A developmental movement education and skill-themes framework.* New York: Routledge.

Graham, G., Holt-Hale, S., McEwen, T., & Parker, M. (1980). *Children moving: A reflective approach to teaching physical education.* New York: McGraw-Hill.

McCarthy, K., Brady, M., & Hallman, K. (2016). *Investigating when it counts: Reviewing the evidence and charting a course of research and action for very young adolescents.* Population Council.

Mertens, S. B., & Caskey, S. M. (Eds). (2018). *Literature reviews in support of the middle level education research agenda.* Charlotte, NC: Information Age Publishing.

Subramaniam, P. R., & Silverman, S. (2007). Middle school students' attitudes toward physical education. *Teaching and Teacher Education, 23*(5).

1

A Review of Movement Education and Skill Themes: What Does It Have to Do with Middle School Physical Education?

Key Concepts:

- ♦ Movement education concepts, and sub-concepts, within the four themes of awareness, are modifiers of movement skills.
- ♦ Skill themes are fundamental motor skills taught using the skill themes approach, which differs from teaching in units. Skill themes are skills that use similar motor patterns.
- ♦ Lesson plans for movement education and skill themes have student learning objectives using psychomotor, cognitive, and affective domains.
- ♦ Transfer of learning is a main reason to teach using the skill themes approach.

- To ensure covering content, effectively keep track of time spent teaching the various concepts and skills by using the "minutes sheets."
- Scaffolding and progressions are an important part of teaching.

A short review of movement education and (sport) skill themes is necessary here to differentiate these models/approaches from how most physical education teachers teach (Graham, Holt-Hale, McEwen, & Parker, 1980). The majority of elementary physical education teachers teach movement and sport skills by units, which is typically referred to as the multi-activity approach, rather than by themes (e.g., hop, jump, etc.), dances (e.g., line/square, etc.), sport skills, and sports. They usually do this once yearly in a series of lessons. The sport skill lessons taught in the multi-activity approach are often seasonally (climate) based, and teachers may use the same equipment for each grade. This can be convenient for the instructor, but may not be developmentally appropriate for all students.

Movement Education

Movement education provides the background knowledge for which to apply to skill themes. You should note that movement education lessons do not contain "sport skill" terminology, but rather general wording. The terms are concepts that are divided into four major themes of awareness: body, space, and effort awareness, and movement quality. For example, a Kindergarten lesson on body awareness might involve asking children to solve the following problem (using divergent or problem-solving methodology): *Can you move a ball on the floor with your foot*? Normally, one might use the word "dribble." However, the author's philosophy is to focus on the concept – in this case, *body awareness*. Therefore, a child "moving" the ball with his/her heel or toe is solving the problem equally successfully as the child who is using their instep. Though the instep might be considered normal or more effective in soccer, it is not the only "solution" to the movement problem. This type of movement education lesson creates the foundation for the skill theme lesson. (See below for movement education concepts.)

Movement Education Concepts

within the 4 major themes (themes are underlined)

Body Awareness:	Levels:	Forces, Create/Absorb:
Body Parts: Head, neck, …	High level	Creating force
	Low level	Absorbing force
Body Surfaces:	Medium level	Transfer of force
		Friction
Flat surface	*Range:*	Gravity
Bumpy surface		Inflicting a force
Large surface	Range	Soft force
Small surface	Range of success	Hard force
Hairy surface	Range of motion	Generate force
Pointed surface		Explosive force
Round surface	Pathways:	Direct force
		Indirect force
Body Shapes:	Curved	On center
	Straight	Off center
Long/thin	Zig zag	Spin
Small/round		Rotate
Creative shapes	Planes:	
		Quality of Movement
Relationships:	Frontal	
	Sagittal	Flow:
Close to	Transverse	
Far from	Along a plane	Bound flow
Bigger	Crossing a plane	Smooth flow
Smaller		Float
	Effort Awareness	Glide
Man. of Objects:		
	Transfer of Weight:	Movement Sequence:
Manipulate		
In control	Heavy	Putting together
Loss of control	Light	Short sequence
	Disperse weight	Long sequence
Space Awareness:	Distribute weight	Transition
Division of Space:	Balance:	Other:
Self space	All forces equal	Angle
Open space		Right angle
General space	Speed:	Parallel
Safe space		Muscles
Invasion of space	Fast	Locomotor
Safe self space	Slow	Nonlocomotor
	Super slow motion	Roll

(Continued)

(*Continued*)

Body Awareness:	Levels:	Forces, Create/Absorb:
Directions:	Medium speed	Thin
	Accelerate	Wide
Forward	Decelerate	Bases of support
Backward		Explore
Sideways	Rhythm:	Mirroring
Left		Copying
Right	Even rhythm	Different
Up	Uneven rhythm	Create
Down		Lead/follow

How to Use the Movement Education Approach

Following what was said earlier about teaching the concepts in "non-consecutive" fashion, the following sheets demonstrate a couple of important items. First, it shows the breakdown of what percentage of the school year's available time in minutes should be allotted to each concept. The percentage of time within each major theme for the grades progresses, with Kindergarten receiving more body awareness lessons and 3rd grade receiving a greater number of movement quality lessons. The movement quality lessons are a more advanced, involved, or complicated category of concepts due to the integration of the other three major themes with progressions.

The teacher records the number of minutes that are taught in each concept on the Minutes sheets. Sample Kindergarten minute sheets are below. The first shows how, if the teacher taught a lesson on how to move safely using the **concept of general space (Division of space is the sub-concept)**, to record it as lesson 1 (Sept 6) and 20 minutes of the 185 minutes allotted for the year.

A Review of Movement Education and Skill Themes ◆ 9

Movement Education Minutes (Kindergarten) Sheet 1

1800 min	60 classes × 30 min	Pct	Min		Kindergarten		Example 1				
				6-Sep							
Body Awareness		32	616	1	2	3	4	5	6	7	
	Body parts	15	92								
	Body surfaces	15	92								
	Body shapes	10	62								
	Body Relationships	30	185								
	Manipulation of objects	30	185								
Space Awareness		32	616								
	Division of space	30	185	20							
	Directions	25	154								
	Levels	25	154								
	Range	5	31								
	Pathways	12	74								
	Planes	3	18								
Effort Awareness		20	385								
	Transfer of weight	20	77								
	Balance	20	77								
	Speed	20	77								
	Rhythm	10	38								
	Creating force	15	58								
	Absorbing force	15	58								
Quality of Movement		10	192								
	Flow	50	96								
	Movement Sequence	50	96								
Miscellaneous		6	116								

Next, on September 9, the teacher taught 25 minutes of a completely different concept, Body Parts. It was recorded as such in the column. Then, on September 15, the teacher returned to Division of Space and "scaffolded," or built on, the previous two lessons, teaching 15 minutes on it, while also covering body parts again for 10 minutes. This is how the minutes are kept and makes it easy to track your teaching of the concepts.

Movement Education Minutes (Kindergarten) Sheet 2

1800 min	*60 classes × 30 min*	*Pct*	*Min*	*6-Sep*	*9-Sep*	*15-Sep*	*Kinder garten*	*Example 3*
Body Awareness		**32**	**616**	1	**2**	**3**	**4**	**5**
	Body parts	15	92		**25**	**10**		
	Body surfaces	15	92					
	Body shapes	10	62					
	Body Relationships	30	185					
	Manipulation of objects	30	185					
Space Awareness		**32**	**616**					
	Division of space	30	185	**20**		**15**		
	Directions	25	154					
	Levels	25	154					
	Range	5	31					
	Pathways	12	74					
	Planes	3	18					
Effort Awareness		**20**	**385**					
	Transfer of weight	20	77					
	Balance	20	77					
	Speed	20	77					
	Rhythm	10	38					
	Creating force	15	58					
	Absorbing force	15	58					
Quality of Movement		**10**	**192**					
	Flow	50	96					
	Movement Sequence	50	96					
Miscellaneous			6	116				

Skill Themes

Skill themes are fundamental motor patterns that are used in games, gymnastics and sports. These patterns are combined into more specialized skills once the basic motor skills become automatic. Schmidt's (1975) schema theory suggests that repeating, or revisiting, a skill in different contexts allows for skill transfer due to the similarity in motor patterns. In other words, lessons on the skill of throwing with a round ball would be done several times yearly in different contexts, such as simply throwing to a target or partner, or throwing for distance. These lessons would *not* be consecutive when using the skill themes approach but might be weeks or months apart. Throwing with oblong balls, such as footballs, is also taught using similar activities, because throwing an oblong ball uses the same basic motor pattern as throwing the round ball. More examples would include a baseball swing and a two-handed tennis backhand, and a soccer or basketball dribble. In the case of the dribble, it is more of a concept than an execution being taught. That is, the student keeping the ball close and under control is the objective.

The rationale for beginning the use of the skill themes approach in, perhaps 4th grade, is that, according to *Paediatrics & Child Health* (2005), certain motor/cognitive skills should not be expected by most children until the age of at least seven. These would include:

- ◆ Increased coordination for catching and throwing
- ◆ Being able to participate in active games with rules
- ◆ Performing sequential motor activities, such as gymnastics or shooting baskets.
- ◆ Improved reaction time in responding to thrown balls.

Therefore, in roughly 4th grade, most students will find the skills and concepts relatable, understandable, and doable. It is now where the wording being used is of both sport skill and strategy terminology (see below). For example, the broad umbrella of "manipulation of objects" encompasses "self-manipulation," "throw/catch/control," "accuracy and power," and "eye-body coordination." Hockey stick handling and lacrosse cradle skills would fall into the theme of "throw/catch/control." Other authors may use different terminology such as "sending/ receiving" for "throw/catch/control." The latter manner is cleaner. The key is to focus on one aspect of, and isolate, a skill when teaching it during a lesson rather than integrating it into a full-sided competitive game.

SKILL THEMES at a Glance

Manipulation of Objects	*Communication and Teamwork*
Self manipulation: Soccer dribble Hockey stick handling Basketball dribbling Lacrosse Cradling	Terms: Common to many sports Specific to sports 　Football: patterns 　Soccer: Square in, man on, etc. 　Plays: volleyball, basketball, etc.
Throw/Catch/Control: Soccer trap/throw in Hockey pass/control Basketball pass/catch Football pass/catch Baseball throw/catch	Forces in sport Absorbing: 　Receiving objects 　Controlling the body Creating: 　Starting movement 　Power skills
Accuracy & Power: Soccer shots Hockey shots Basketball shots Lacrosse Football place kick/punt	Transferring: 　From body to object 　Person to person Manipulation of: 　Spins on objects 　Body position
Eye-body part coordination Baseball hitting Tennis Volleyball skills Badminton Basic eye-body part activities Movement & Position in space Offensive: 　Creating spaces 　Position and support of teammates 　Speed and direction change 　Fakes, fades, dodging 　See your teammate	Quality of movement: Flow 　Smooth 　Correct form
Defensive: 　Guarding 　Position and support 　Tackling and tagging 　Interception/blocking 　Stay between opponent and goal	

How to Use the Skill Themes Approach

The tracking of the minutes taught for each skill theme is done in a very similar fashion. Below is a sample Minutes page for 4th Grade. Notice that the teacher chose to teach a basketball dribble (**within the theme of object manipulation, sub-theme self-manipulation**) for 15 minutes on the first day of class.

Skill Themes Minutes (4th Grade) Sheet 1

Class:		Grade 4		Example 1
				18-Sep
Manipulation of Objects	Pct	Min		1
Self manipulation	13	162		
Soccer Dribble				
Hockey Stick Handling				
Basketball Dribble				15
Lacrosse Cradle				
Throw/Catch/Control	8	100		
Soccer trap/throw-in				
Hockey pass/control				
Basketball pass/catch				
Lacrosse pass/catch				
Football pass/catch				
Baseball throw/catch				
Accuracy and Power	8	100		
Soccer				
shots				
Hockey shots				
Basketball shots				
Lacrosse shots				
Football place kick/				
punt				
Eye Body Part Control	8	100		
Baseball hitting				
Tennis				
Volleyball				
Badminton				
Movement/Position in Space				
Offensive	19	237		
Creating space				
Position and support				
Speed/Direction change				
Fake/Fade/Dodge				
See your teammate				

(Continued)

14 ◆ A Review of Movement Education and Skill Themes

(*Continued*)

Class:		Grade 4		Example 1
				18-Sep
Defensive		**14**	175	
	Guarding			
	Position and support			
	Tackling and tagging			
	Intercept/Blocking			
	Goaltending angle			
	Keep betw opp/goal			
Communication and Teamwork		**10**	125	
Terms				
	Common to sport			
	Specific to sport			
	Patterns/plays			
Cooperative Games		**15**	187	
		15	294	
Forces in sport		**5**	63	
Absorption of				
	Receive object			
	Land/Control body			
Creating				
	Start movement			
	Power skills			
Transferring				
	Body to object			
	Person to person			
Manipulation of				
	Spins on object			
	Body position			

Then, on September 22, the teacher decided to do a lesson on baseball throwing or catching (likely with a tennis ball). It is recorded as such. You likely see the sequence. **Vary** the skills, **revisit** them it in different contexts, **scaffold**, and **progress**! Tracking your minutes really helps both you, and the variety helps the students develop.

A Review of Movement Education and Skill Themes ◆ 15

Skill Themes Minutes (4th Grade) Sheet 2

Class:			Grade 4		Example 1	
					18-Sep	22-Sep
Manipulation of Objects		**Pct**	**Min**		**1**	**2**
Self manipulation		**13**	162			
	Soccer Dribble					
	Hockey Stick Handling					
	Basketball Dribble				15	
	Lacrosse Cradle					
Throw/Catch/Control		**8**	100			
	Soccer trap/throw-in					
	Hockey pass/control					
	Basketball pass/catch					
	Lacrosse pass/catch					
	Football pass/catch					
	Baseball throw/catch					20
Accuracy and Power		**8**	100			
	Soccer shots					
	Hockey shots					
	Basketball shots					
	Lacrosse shots					
	Football place kick/punt					
Eye Body Part Control		**8**	100			
	Baseball hitting					
	Tennis					
	Volleyball					
	Badminton					
Movement/Position in Space						
Offensive		**19**	237			
	Creating space					
	Position and support					
	Speed/Direction change					
	Fake/Fade/Dodge					
	See your teammate					
Defensive		**14**	175			
	Guarding					
	Position and support					
	Tackling and tagging					
	Intercept/Blocking					
	Goaltending angle					
	Keep between opp/goal					

(Continued)

16 ◆ A Review of Movement Education and Skill Themes

(*Continued*)

Class:		Grade 4		*Example 1*	
				18-Sep	22-Sep
Communication and Teamwork		10	125		
Terms					
	Common to sport				
	Specific to sport				
	Patterns/plays				
Cooperative Games		15	187		
		15	294		
Forces in sport		5	63		
Absorption of					
	Receive object				
	Land/Control body				
Creating					
	Start movement				
	Power skills				
Transferring					
	Body to object				
	Person to person				
Manipulation of					
	Spins on object				
	Body position				

Lesson Plans for Movement Education

What follows are a couple of sample lesson plans for movement education. The first one is a beginner lesson on body parts, within the major theme of body awareness. Notice it is for grades K-3, and is labeled as a beginner lesson. This could indicate it is for a Kindergarten class, or for a 3rd grade class that has not had a background in this material. More on that will be covered in the next chapter.

Notice that for all of the lessons, fitness is not directly included. This is purposeful. The LTL that you see in the warm-up section means "line-to-line." In my teaching I would give students a movement problem to solve as they entered class, often based on the previous class. They would then move from one gymnasium line (the one they entered class on) to another (a short distance) and back. During this moving they would be solving the problem. As an example, "go 3 times LTL while facing a different direction each time." The fitness that is attained during the year in physical education class in this program is derived from their movement throughout the entire lesson, not just this brief warm-up (or what some might refer to as an "instant activity"). In a good, quality program, with enough equipment for all students to be active at all times, general fitness can be obtained. However, it is philosophically not measured or assessed at this level.

Name _____   LESSON PLAN

Domains_____   Objectives (for this lesson)_____   Date:____

Physical	To place different body parts on floor inside hoop	Grade: K-3 **Beg**
Cognitive	To name body parts	Theme: Body Awareness Concept: Body parts
Cognitive		Equipment: Hula hoops
Affective	To play by rules/cooperatively	Reference

CONTENT	ORGANIZATION AND TRANSITION	TEACHING PROGRESSION AND TEACHING CUES	EVALUATION, MODIFICATION, SUGGESTIONS (per objective)
Warm-up:	LTL Self space	3 × facing a different direction each time	
Focus:	Hula hoops placed on floor **equidistantly** Each student assigned to a hoop to begin by sitting inside of.	"We are going to explore many body parts we have! Upon signal, stand and travel (perhaps provide a locomotor movement) all over the area by yourself. When asked to stop, find your hoop and place a body part down inside of it." This continues.	
Medial Summary	Their hoops	Point out that some children were using "common" parts of their body (hand), while others were using different (back, head). Both are fine. Encourage the use of creativity. Encourage them to name the body part they put on the floor each time.	
Review:	Circle	Questions to ask: Who would like to demonstrate what they did? Name some parts.	

Sample Lesson plan #2 for K-3. Notice that it is an intermediate lesson. This plan could be for a Kindergarten toward the end of the year, or a beginning of the year 3rd grade class.

Name _____   LESSON PLAN

Domains_____ Objectives (for this lesson)_____ Date:____

Physical	To land a scarf on various body parts	Grade: K-3 **Int**
Cognitive	To have awareness of body parts	Themes: Body Awareness Concept: Body parts
Cognitive		Equipment: scarves
Affective	To play game safely and cooperatively	Reference

CONTENT	ORGANIZATION AND TRANSITION	TEACHING PROGRESSION AND TEACHING CUES	EVALUATION, MODIFICATION, SUGGESTIONS (per objective)
Warm-up:	In on line LTL		

(*Continued*)

CONTENT	ORGANIZATION AND TRANSITION	TEACHING PROGRESSION AND TEACHING CUES	EVALUATION, MODIFICATION, SUGGESTIONS (per objective)
Focus:	Children are given scarves and asked to find self space.	Review of body parts. Problem given: Upon signal travel with the scarf in your hand. Upon different signal, stop and toss the scarf in the air, and have it LAND (come to rest) on a body part of your choice. Repeat this task several times. Encourage several ways.	
Medial Summary	Self space	Encourage students to call out the name of the part it lands on. If the concept of "levels" has been taught, students can be asked to have it land on an "upper body part" or "lower body part." Modification: In partners, travel together and upon signal tosses it in the air for the OTHER partner to have it land on.	
Review:	Collect scarves Circle	Name parts the scarf landed on. What did you have to do with your body to have it land on your: hand, elbow, knee, bottom of foot, back, etc.?	

This sample lesson plan's theme is on body awareness, and the concept is shapes.

Name _____   LESSON PLAN

Domains_____ Objectives (for this lesson)_____ Date:_____

Physical	To create different body shapes	Grade: K-2
Cognitive	To recognize shapes	Theme: Body Concept: shapes
Cognitive	To know rules of game	Equipment: foam shapes
Affective	To play game by the rules/to work together	Reference

CONTENT	ORGANIZATION AND TRANSITION	TEACHING PROGRESSION AND TEACHING CUES	EVALUATION, MODIFICATION, SUGGESTIONS *(per objective)*
Warm-up:	Attendance Circle Self space	Review of previous lesson: Tunnel Tag using speeds: run slow/save those who are frozen by running fast; run fast/save slow.	
Focus:	Self space	A review of "body shapes" – wide, round, etc. Move around area changing shapes while using bound flow (K-1), 2nd grade will do same in groups of 3, creating "dance" of like shapes simultaneously. A few demonstrations first by volunteers.	
Medial Summary Review:	Self space	Where might you see this activity?	

Lesson Plans for Skill Themes

What follows are a couple of lesson plans for use in the 4th or 5th grades. The warm-up is once again left to the teacher. However, now basic fitness activities can be incorporated along with knowledge of the health-fitness components. Examples can include jumping rope, jogging around, stretching, push-ups, etc. It should be the students' choice at this age. Much more on fitness for middle school will be covered in the Fitness chapter.

The first lesson plan shows soccer dribbling with the theme of Manipulation of Objects, and the sub-theme is Self-Manipulation. The second sample lesson is the same major theme of Manipulation of Objects, but the sub-theme is Throw/Catch/Control. The third lesson has the same major theme and sub-theme as the first, but uses a different object, and therefore demonstrates how the sub-theme (of control) carries over.

**The teacher should also be aware that the movement concepts are considered modifiers for the sport skills. You'll recall that the basketball dribble is continuously manipulated from medium level to low level and back. Medium and low (levels) can be considered the modifiers for where the skill (the basketball dribble) is taking place.

Name _____   LESSON PLAN

Domains_____ Objectives (for this lesson)_____ Date:____

Physical	To dribble a soccer ball under control; around defender	Grade: 4–5 **int**
Cognitive	To know how maneuver around defender	Theme: Manipulation Sub-Theme: Self-manipulation soccer dribble
Cognitive		Equipment: soccer balls
Affective	To allow self to help partner	Reference

CONTENT	ORGANIZATION AND TRANSITION	TEACHING PROGRESSION AND TEACHING CUES	EVALUATION, MODIFICATION, SUGGESTIONS (per objective)
Warm-up: **Focus**:	**Each** student starts with a ball. X X X X X	Problem: dribble your soccer ball in s straight pathway making as many touches of the ball as you can at progressively faster speeds and STOP ball (with your foot) at the line. Repeat 3–4 times.	

(*Continued*)

CONTENT	ORGANIZATION AND TRANSITION	TEACHING PROGRESSION AND TEACHING CUES	EVALUATION, MODIFICATION, SUGGESTIONS (per objective)
Medial Summary Brief review	Students with balls Defenders X ⟹ ⟸ X X ⟹ ⟸ X X ⟹ ⟸ X Return equipment	How far did the ball travel away from you as you did this…close or far? (Should be close). Next: in partners, only 1 ball per pair. Face each other from opposite ends. Student with ball is dribbler, does same as before. Defender, though, approaches but at VARIABLE speed. Dribbler must try to maneuver around and past defender and back into the pathway to get **1 point**. **DEFENDER MAY NOT TOUCH THE BALL.** Make sure there is enough room between pairs to allow for safety when they go around partner.	
Review:		How did you maneuver around? How far is the ball from you when you went around? What parts of your foot were you using to dribble? To change its direction? What other skills would use this concept? (hockey stick handling, basketball dribble)	

Name _____   LESSON PLAN

Domains_____ Objectives (for this lesson)_____ Date:____

Physical	Throw/**catch** to catch ball into mitt from increased distances	Grade: 4–5 **Beg**
Cognitive	Throw/**Catch** to know technique of catching	Theme: Manipulation Sub-Theme: Throw/catch/control (catch)
Cognitive		Equipment: baseball mitts, softballs
Affective	To work willingly with partner	Reference

CONTENT	*ORGANIZATION AND TRANSITION*	*TEACHING PROGRESSION AND TEACHING CUES*	*EVALUATION, MODIFICATION, SUGGESTIONS (per objective)*
Warm-up: **Focus**:	Divide into partners, all get mitts and find a space facing a wall, making sure they have self-space.	Personal warm-up Students will warm-up individually by tossing the ball against the wall and catching their own ball. Ask students to vary how they catch the ball.	

(Continued)

CONTENT	ORGANIZATION AND TRANSITION	TEACHING PROGRESSION AND TEACHING CUES	EVALUATION, MODIFICATION, SUGGESTIONS (per objective)
Medial Summary Brief review	Children will now find a partner, facing each other from a short distance apart. ◄X ⟷x ⟶ ◄ X ⟷x ⟶	Play "Giant Step Catch": partners are to toss the ball to each other. Each time a ball is caught, the catcher takes 1 giant step backwards, thereby increasing the distance between partners. If they reach the safe boundary line, they can continue to reverse the distance. Change the activity to "Consecutive Throws" to see how many consecutive catches can be made from a set distance of student choice. Discuss catching technique…with student demonstrations.	
Review:	Return equipment	Which methods give the most chance of success in catching? (2 hands, mitt up/down depending on level of catch), squeeze ball.	

Name _____   LESSON PLAN

Domains_____ Objectives (for this lesson)_____ Date:____

Physical	To maintain control of dribbling a basketball while traveling with distractions	Grade: 4–5 **adv**
Cognitive	To know how to adjust factors (hand positioning, etc.) for the dribble	Theme: Manipulation Sub-Theme: Self-manipulation basketball dribble
Cognitive		Equipment: basketballs, scooters
Affective	To play cooperatively	Reference

CONTENT	ORGANIZATION AND TRANSITION	TEACHING PROGRESSION AND TEACHING CUES	EVALUATION, DIFICATION, SUGGESTIONS (per objective)

Warm-up:
Focus:
	Each student starts with a ball. 3–5 scooters for a class of 20.
	
	     D
	       I
	   D
	        D
	    D
	  I D
	D= dribbler
	I= "invader," student on scooter
		All but 3–5 children start with a ball in a self-space. The 3–5 children are sitting on scooters and are considered the "invaders."
		Problem: Using what has been previously taught regarding dribbling, children are to dribble about the area maintaining control. The invaders attempt, with their feet, to push balls away from the dribblers. If someone loses control of their dribble, they go to a designated area to practice the skill of dribbling with each hand for a designated amount of time. Invaders should be rotated.	

(Continued)

(*Continued*)

CONTENT	ORGANIZATION AND TRANSITION	TEACHING PROGRESSION AND TEACHING CUES	EVALUATION, DIFICATION, SUGGESTIONS (*per objective*)
Medial **Summary** Brief review **Review**:		Think about what factors or concepts help you to control the ball. Rotate invaders often. How did you maneuver around? What were some factors? (speed, level of dribble, directions of travel, etc.) What other skills would use this concept? (hockey stick handling, soccer dribble)	

Chapter 1 Review

You should now:

- have general knowledge of movement education concepts, and sub-concepts, within the 4 themes of awareness.
- have general knowledge of what skill themes are, and how teaching using skill themes differs from teaching by units.
- know that the movement concepts are the modifiers for the movement skills.
- have an idea of what lesson plans for movement education and skill themes look like and be able to create your own.

Reading Comprehension Questions

1. List three movement education concepts within each of the four themes of awareness? List two sub-concepts under each of the concepts.
2. You want your 10-year-olds to gain some experience in moving quickly and safely through limited space. Using the movement education model, how would you phrase a movement problem for these children? Would it use direct or indirect methodology?
3. What is another way, other than asking students to dribble, to have your 11-year-olds work with the concept of "levels" while using a bouncy ball? Does it matter, for this purpose, the number of hands they use? Why or why not?
4. Which of the four major themes contains the most advanced or involved category of concepts due to the integration of the other three major themes with progressions? How do the use of scaffolding and progressions build into this theme?
5. Of a baseball throw, a soccer dribble, and a hockey pass, which one does NOT fit into the theme of "throw/catch/control?" Which theme *does* your answer fit into?

6. How will you know when you have enough of a particular concept or skill when using the Minutes Sheets?
7. For both the movement education and Skill Themes approaches, what is the biggest deviation from the more traditional models, with respect to the sequencing of the lessons?
8. What three objectives could you create (one for each psychomotor, cognitive, and affective domains) for teaching a lesson on *body parts* using the movement education approach?
9. What three objectives could you create for teaching a lesson on the volleyball overhand serve using the skill themes approach?

References

Graham, G., Holt-Hale, S., McEwen, T., & Parker, M. (1980) *Children moving: A reflective approach to teaching physical education.* New York: McGraw-Hill.

Schmidt, R. A. (1975). A schema theory of discreet motor skill learning. *Psychological Review, 82*(4).

2

The Sport Education Model ...and How to Progress to It from Chapter 1

Why Did We Need Chapter 1? What Does it Have to Do with Middle School Physical Education?

Key Concepts:

- ♦ The foundation created by teaching movement education concepts and sport skill themes assists in learning sport skills more deeply
- ♦ Middle school aged students vary greatly in their sport skills, so the amount or percentage of lessons taught using movement education and skill themes sill be up to the teacher.
- ♦ "Concept transfer" assists in motor patterns, aiding the stronger learning of sports skills.
- ♦ Sport Education is a progressive model used to teach Physical Education, and uses Captain's Packets and student workbooks. Every student has a role in this model.

Situation: You, the middle school physical education teacher, are beginning the school year. You are aware that the 5th or 6th grade students were not, in their previous school's physical education class, taught via movement education. You also know that, though they did learn sport skills in their elementary school, they were not taught the sport skills using the skill themes approach. Translation: the students may not have the knowledge of movement efficiency or movement vocabulary (the concepts) as you would have hoped, and their sport skills, though perhaps normal for their age, may not be as fluid as you hoped.

We know that there are always going to be some children in any given class that are strong at sport skills, and some who are not as strong. We know that parental influence is a factor, just like there are many other factors. So what can you do to remedy this and prepare them for a higher level of proficiency, that which they should gain in your teaching at the middle school?

How Much Movement Education and Skill Themes Should Be Taught? Preparing for the Transition to Sport Education

One option of preparing the middle school students for Sport Education is to infuse lessons of the variety that were presented in Chapter 1. Granted, 10- and 11-year-olds can move (they are active)! However, by sharing with the students, at the beginning of the year, the rationale behind doing some movement "exploration," as well as reinforcing some basic sport skills, you are likely to find students receptive. It's all in the presentation, of course. The teacher's challenge will be to find a middle ground in terms of the number of lessons that will be needed to reach or impact all students. It is teacher discretion to determine when the students understand the concepts.

Further, and more importantly, the **wording** being used during these movement education lessons (the concepts) is crucial. Students may be able to, for example, dribble a basketball to a good degree. However, are they aware of the "levels" that they are using? During the dribble, the basketball is being manipulated (purposefully used word) in space by the student from a medium level to a low level and back to a medium level, repetitively. Likewise, are the students able to move, or travel, in different "pathways?" In a tagging game, they are doing just that, constantly moving in zig-zag pathways (and others), while in a soccer dribble they are often moving, or manipulating, the ball in a zig-zag pathway. The more terminology the teacher can infuse the better. An experienced teacher would likely have a Word Wall in the gymnasium.

Another good way to explain to the students the value of learning the concepts and themes is Schmidt's (1975) theory of concept transfer that is used in relating movement concepts to skills. On the Concept Transfer chart (page 34), you can see several examples of how the concepts learned are used in actual sport skills. The left column indicates the major theme addressed. The middle column shows how the concept within the theme is addressed. The right hand column gives a couple of specific sport examples.

Examples of Concept Transfer

From James Rose

THEME →	CONCEPT →	SPORT EXAMPLE
Body Awareness	Large, flat surfaces increase object control	– short soccer pass (instep pass rather than laces)
Effort Awareness	The wider the base of support, the more stability produced Increasing the number of points of the base also increases stability	– wrestling – gymnastics
Body/Effort	Continuous object control is more difficult at higher speeds	– soccer dribbling – basketball dribbling – hockey stick handling
Effort Awareness	A force placed off-center to an object causes rotation of the object	– baseball pitching – soccer shot – volleyball serve – bowling
Space Awareness	Objects following a zig-zag pathway are harder to control and predict or track	– soccer dribbling – hockey stick handling
Effort/Body Awareness	Force absorption by the body Is best done be joint flexion	– gymnastics – wrestling

Dr. Michael Gosset Yonkers PE Workshop 2015

The methodology, or pedagogical approach, used to teach these lessons should be of the indirect style. Mosston and Ashworth's Spectrum of Teaching Styles (1994) has several styles. Within the indirect category are exploration (for movement education) and problem-solving (for the skill themes approach). In brief, the indirect approach has the teacher pose a movement problem to the class. The students then "experiment" and try to find various solutions to this problem, for which there is certainly more than one. For the problem-solving style, the teacher asks students to also find a solution to a movement problem, but shifts to a *guided discovery* methodology. This method guides students toward a solution. An example might be asking students how they can achieve their furthest one handed throw of a ball. Some children may use the same side foot and arm, and some might use opposition. By guiding students toward a developmentally appropriate solution, they are learning by what is comfortable for them. By using these styles, children will internalize solutions better as they create, as opposed to responding to the command style, which is a direct approach.

As the children are exposed to several of these lessons, especially the skill-themed ones, they should develop the "muscle memory" of motor patterns. Examples mentioned earlier are the baseball swing and the two-handed backhand. With the general motor patterns somewhat ingrained, it will be time to transition to the learning of sport skills more seriously. Now is the time to implement the Sport Education model.

Sport Education

Sport Education Defined and Explained

Purpose

Daryl Siedentop brought the Sport Education model of physical education to the United States in the early 1990's. His goal of this model was to have students become "competent, literate, and enthusiastic sportspersons" (Siedentop, 1994, p. 4). This model differs from traditional models due to the extended length of time that a sport is covered (taught). Traditionally, teaching sports in school is based on the time of year, often to correspond to popular interscholastic sports. For example, in most locales, football and volleyball are almost always in the Fall, basketball and wrestling are almost always in the Winter, and baseball and golf are almost always in the Spring. The sports of soccer, tennis, lacrosse, and others vary, often based on the geographic location the school. Alaska's sports program timetable may differ from Florida's! Again, the physical education program's curricular offerings are often dictated by this. Therefore, in order to be able to teach all of these sports, the time period devoted to each becomes somewhat limited.

Overall Implementation and Roles

Sport Education, however, is structured to use what are called "seasons." Each season could be perhaps as long as two to three months. This length provides the opportunity to have a more in-depth learning of the sport, or what Siedentop calls *authenticity*. This learning includes the rules and history of the sport, selected skills, and possibly strategies. (Later in this chapter you will learn about beginning, and advanced versions.) A significant aspect of Sport Education is the use of the many roles students assume. Roles include captain, sportswriter, statistician, scorekeeper, equipment manager, and official. (It is often wise to have more than one student for each role in case of student absence.) The teacher can add more, such as fitness coach. If you are sensing a pattern, yes, this does wonders for student ownership on a team. A student who enjoys math is likely to volunteer to be statistician, and the one who likes to write may want to be sportswriter. Each role comes with its own responsibility sheet describing what to do. This structure also contributes to socio-emotional learning, and the affective domain. Even more value-laden is that students cooperatively think of a team name and team color. This addresses the *affiliation* aspect of this model.

Preseason

Every member of a team receives a multi-page student workbook (teacher created) for a given sport that is being taught. This workbook (page 38) includes the rules and history of the sport with review questions, the specific skills to be learned, their explanation and rubrics for assessment, diagrams for positioning, and more. The student is responsible for completing all of the information and signing their workbook. (Workbooks for two other sports are available from the support material at www.routledge.com/9781032698366.)

Physical Education

UNDERSTANDING

Volleyball

From James W. Rose

This workbook belongs to

Student: _____

School-year: _____

Volleyball History

The modern sport of volleyball was created by the physical director of a Y.M.C.A. in Massachusetts. William G. Morgan invented this sport in 1895. He thought this game would be more appealing to those who could not keep up with other, more vigorous, sports. Mr. Morgan originally called this sport Mintonette. However, the following year a man named Alfred Halstead renamed the game, because he felt that the title Volleyball more accurately characterized the skills of the game.

In the year 1900, the first official rules were written. Throughout the years, the rules of volleyball have changed. They were revised in 1912. This revision established areas such as the serve, the rotation, and the 15-point game.

During the 20th century, the popularity of volleyball increased. Early in the century, South America and Canada became active in the sport. As time went on, the rest of the world became interested in it. This popularity led volleyball to its first Olympic Games in 1968 in Tokyo, Japan.

Now, volleyball is played recreationally and competitively all around the world.

Basic Rules of Volleyball

The objective of volleyball is to hit the ball over the net and into the opponents' area in a way such that they cannot return it, thereby scoring a point. At one point in time, only the team serving could gain a point. Now, however, rally scoring is in place and a team can win a point whether they are serving or not.

A volleyball court is 60 feet long and 30 feet wide. The court is divided by a net that is 8 feet high for men, and 7 feet 4 ½ inches for women.

Two teams of six play on opposite sides of the net. Each team may only touch the ball at most 3 times before returning it over the net. A block by a player at the net does not count as a hit.

40 ◆ The Sport Education Model…and How to Progress to It from Chapter 1

The game ends when one team scores 25 points. The winning team must win by at least 2 points, or unlimited overtime occurs to reach a 2-point margin.

The most common infractions (fouls) are when players catch, "carry," or lift the ball instead of hitting it. This results in a point for the other team.

In addition, the net may not be touched, nor can a player go under the net. At one time, a serve that touched the net was out of play (and loss of point), but recently a serve that touches the net and goes over it is still in play.

History and Rules Comprehension

Submit the answers 2 class periods after your team learns and discusses the history and rules in class.

1. Who invented the sport of volleyball? _____

2. What was volleyball's original name? _____

3. Why did Alfred Halstead rename this sport? _____
   _____

4. When was the first original set of rules drawn up?
   _____

5. What year did volleyball become an Olympic event?
   _____

6. How many players are on the court for one team?
   _____

7. Name 2 ways a volleyball game may end.

   a) _____

   b) _____

Volleyball Player Positioning

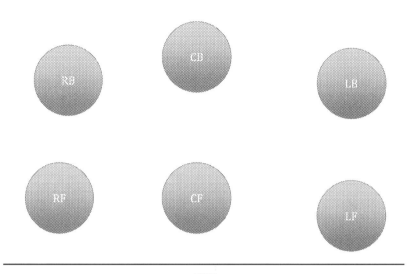

NET

LF = left forward
CF = center forward
RF = right forward

LB = left back
CB = center back
RB = right back

usually responsible for:
1. Setting the ball
2. Spiking the ball
3. Blocking the spike

usually responsible for:
1. Forearm passing or digging
2. Setting the ball
3. RB is responsible for serving, but can serve from anywhere behind the back line.

The Rotation in Volleyball

Whenever a non-serving team wins the serve, a rotation must occur by having each player on this team move clockwise around the court. This is illustrated below:

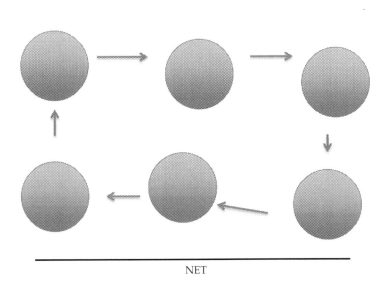

NET

Position and Rotation Comprehension

Submit the answers 2 class periods after your team discusses the positions and rotation in class.

1. How many players are in the front row? _____

2. What positions are responsible for the most sets and spikes? _____

   _____

3. Which position is the server? _____

4. What positions usually forearm pass or dig? _____

5. If you are a left forward, what position would you play after rotating?

   _____

Skill Activity #1

The Forearm Pass

The forearm pass is **usually** the first hit by a team, though recent rule changes have permitted the set to be as well. The objective of the forearm pass is to pass the ball to someone who can set the ball for a front row player to spike. A common pattern of forearm pass, set, and spike occurs for both teams.

I CAN TAKE NOTES HERE

Skill Awareness I

1. When executing the forearm pass, your fingers can be locked, but your thumbs must be _____

2. It is important for your thumbs to be directly _____ the ball.

3. Your elbows should be _____

4. Your knees should be _____

5. After contact, your legs should _____

6. What large muscle gives you your lift on a forearm pass? _____

Skill Activity #2

The Set

The set is a very important shot in volleyball. The objective is to set the ball high and close to the net, "setting" up your teammate for a spike.

I CAN TAKE NOTES HERE

Skill Awareness 2

1. Just before the ball makes contact with the setter, all the setter's joints, including the fingers, should be _____

2. After the set is made, and the setter is now in full extension, _____
_____.

48 ◆ The Sport Education Model...and How to Progress to It from Chapter 1

Skill Activity #3

The spike and the serve

The spike and the serve are probably the two strongest offensive shots. If these skills are perfected, points may come more easily.

I CAN TAKE NOTES HERE

1. Name the two types of serves.

   A _____

   B _____

2. It is important to jump straight _____ when spiking.

3. When spiking, it is important to _____ not to _____.

You Will be Tested on One of the Skills on the Next 2 Pages

THE FOREARM PASS

	POINTS EARNED	POSSIBLE POINTS
Feet slightly spread, one foot front, one back	_____	1 pt
Both knees bent	_____	2 pts
Arms extended, flat surface with arms together	_____	1 pt
Thumbs together	_____	1 pt
When hitting ball, knees extend, arms remain straight	_____	
and extended, angled down	_____	2 pts
"Shoulder shrug" used to maintain straight arms	_____	1 pt
Contact made with forearms	_____	2 pts
TOTAL: (out of 10)	_____	

50 ◆ The Sport Education Model…and How to Progress to It from Chapter 1

THE SET

	POINTS EARNED	POSSIBLE POINTS
Preparation		
Knees flexed	_____	1 pt
Position is under and behind the ball	_____	1 pt
Elbows bent and spread wide	_____	1 pt
Head up and looking through "window"	_____	1 pt
Action		
Knees and elbows extend as ball is hit	_____	2 pts
Contact is made with finger pads	_____	2 pts
Thumb and forefingers together	_____	1 pt
Feet in diagonal position	_____	1 pt

TOTAL: (out of 10) _____

Volleyball Vocabulary

1. ROTATION - _____

   _____

2. THE FOREARM PASS - _____

   _____

3. THE SET - _____

   _____

4. ANAEROBIC - _____

   _____

5. EXTENSION - _____

   _____

6. AGILITY - _____

   _____

7. THE SERVE - _____

   _____

8. WILLIAM MORGAN - _____

   _____

9. ALFRED HALSTEAD

   _____

I believe that volleyball involves mostly _____
fitness.

My reason for my answer is: _____
_____
_____

My volleyball booklet is complete to the **best of my ability**. I understand this booklet and am ready to participate in this sport.

SIGNED: _____

TEACHER'S INITIALS: _____

The Volleyball workbook is just one example of such a workbook. You may use any sport you like to create your own. For example, if you choose Basketball, choices of skills might be the chest pass, the set shot, and the dribble. You would create checklists for cues for each and assign point values adding up to 10 points. You would have a brief history of Basketball, its general rules, and of course, you would create a 10-point quiz. An example of a quiz (this one for Volleyball) is on pages 56–57. The sport(s) you choose don't have to be a team sport. Gymnastics, Track & Field, and Tennis are sports to be used as well. There are books and resources for creating tournaments using these, and other sports.

Captains, Teams, and the Captain's Packet

It is recommended that team captains be selected by the teacher based on their physical education grade. (The grading system will be covered in a later chapter.) The grade may be the most recent test or quiz grade, or an overall grade. Teams can then be created randomly by the teacher. The captain of the team receives a Captain's Packet (p. 63). In this packet, there is a sheet for team members to sign up for the specific roles explained above, and a tentative schedule for the learning and practice parts of the season, the pre-season, and the actual season of competition. It is the captain's responsibility to "check off" each skill as the team completes them. See more on this in the next paragraph.

Of course, the chances are that there will be enough students for more than one team per class. With Sport Education, the teams will be learning the skills and practicing at their own pace. The teacher will likely demonstrate the skills. The captains get to choose, for their respective teams, the order in which they want to learn the material (skills and rules/history). So, if all teams happen to want to learn, for example, a volleyball forearm pass first, then the teacher can demonstrate it. The teams will then go practice on their own. The captain organizes the practices. *One key aspect of the Sport Education model is that the captains monitor the learning.* When a team captain feels all team members are sufficiently competent on skills (via checklist), they can summon the teacher to observe them and see if all members are competent. An example of a partner assessment checklist that can be used by the teams, prior to having the teacher check the team, follows.

54 ◆ The Sport Education Model…and How to Progress to It from Chapter 1

Physical Education

Peer Assessment

Performer_____   Observer _____   Class _____

Date _____

Volleyball Set

Directions:

Performer: Have ball tossed to you 5 times….you "pass" properly to wall

Observer: (+) if this cue is done properly most of the time

(–) if this cue is **not** done properly most of the time

write positive comments at the end

Cues for performer:	*+ or –*
Legs slightly spread, one foot front, one back.	_____
Both knees bent.	_____
Arms overhead, elbows bent and wide, fingers spread.	_____
When touching ball, knees extend.	_____
When touching ball arms extend.	_____
Ball contacted with finger PADS, fingers extended.	_____
Hands finish high in air.	_____

Observer's comments _____

_____

Performer: I feel GOOD/OK/NEED WORK with my serve.

Therefore, when the teacher is called to check the team's skill level, and (s)he believes it is satisfactory, a check is placed by the teacher, and initialed, with the date, on the appropriate page of the Captain's Packet. The team then moves on to another skill. It is, once again, the choice of the team (captain) as to which order to learn or practice. Remember, the captain organizes the practices. When all of the members have been checked off for all items on the sheet, the team has a choice of activities until all teams are ready for the next step. Activity choices can include scrimmaging, practicing individually, or studying the material. It is up to the captain to decide which would be most beneficial.

The Season

The tournament begins once all teams have been checked off on all skills. There is one more caveat here. Assessment in all areas will be covered later in Chapter 5. *However, in order to be considered "eligible" to participate in the season tournament, both a written quiz (often 10 questions) and the skill test are given prior to the season (competition) beginning.* A sample quiz is on page 56. Each team member must get a minimum of seven on the quiz to be eligible for the season's tournament. Additionally, the aggregate score for the team to compete in the tournament must be a minimum of 40. Any points above an aggregate of 70 are counted as bonus points within the tournament. (An uneven number of players on teams, or not exactly ten on a team, would require extrapolation in some way for the teacher to execute.) Anyone scoring below four does have an opportunity to take the quiz again.

Physical Education

Volleyball

Quiz

_____   _____   _____
Name   Team Name   Date

**Place the letter for the correct answer on the line
DO NOT CIRCLE:**

1) _____How many times, at most, can a team legally hit the ball before it goes over the net?
   a) 2   b) 3
   c) 4   d) it doesn't matter

2) _____A hit that prepares the team for a spike is the
   a) forearm pass   b) serve
   c) set   d) dig

3) _____A team rotates positions:
   a) after every point that is played
   b) whenever they want
   c) if they **were** serving and they win the point
   d) if they **were not** serving and they win the point

4) _____The original name of volleyball was
   a) Walleyball   b) Mintonette
   c) netball   d) Rounders

5) _____Volleyball in the Olympic Games started in
   a) 1896   b) 1912
   c) 1968   d) it is not played in Olympics

6) _____When a player sets the ball, (s)he should be
   a) under and in front of the ball
   b) under and behind the ball
   c) over the ball
   d) next to the ball

The Sport Education Model…and How to Progress to It from Chapter 1 ◆ 57

7) _____The arm muscle mostly responsible for the overhand serve is
   a) quadriceps   c) cardiac
   c) tricep   d) gastrocnemius

8) _____ What kind of cardiovascular conditioning is best for volleyball:
   a) aerobic   b) muscular
   c) sleep   d) anaerobic

9) _____ The game of volleyball was created in the state of
   a) New York   b) California
   c) Massachusetts   d) Vermont

10) _____ Players on a team rotate
    a) clockwise
    b) counter-clockwise
    c) back and forth
    d) as assigned by the captain

Regarding the team playing in the tournament, recall that each team member is both a player role and also has a role to fulfill. The equipment manager might supply the balls for the game, as well as collect them afterward. The official might be responsible for making calls during the game. For example, for volleyball, the official might rotate in and out of a linesperson's position. The statistician might record how many successful serves each team member had and make a tally on a posted scoreboard. The scorekeeper would right down the winning team and the scores for each team on the sample scorecard on page 62. Hopefully, each team member is wearing a t-shirt of the color decided on by the team. There are ways of making these classes quite festive, such as a team banner.

As mentioned, due to the nature of the organization of Sport Education, there could be more than two teams. In that case, on any given day, the team that is not scheduled to play would practice on their own, monitored by the teacher. Sometimes, a game will go fast and allow for two games to be played. In this case, the practicing team can now play and one of the teams that was competing becomes the practicing team.

When done comprehensively, a Sport Education season can take more than two months, depending on the class scheduling.

A Sample Sport Education Season Organization

Day 1

(Much of this is repetitive)

After the daily warm-up segment, the teams and captains are presented. The teams are teacher selected. It is recommended that the captains be chosen by the teacher **based on the results their most recent objectively assessed skill or written quizzes.** (Assessment is focused on in Chapter 5.) The teams are given time to choose their team roles, their team name, and their team color.

Days 2–6 (or as many as needed)

Skills, and rules/history learning. Teachers check off each one when complete.

Days 7-??

Pre-season: Informal within-team playing, practicing. Scrimmaging vs. other team is at the discretion of the teacher. If scrimmaging indeed occurs, it is wise to begin emphasizing the affective domain through sportsmanship. A report can be created that assesses this…in this case *self*-assesses it. As is with all areas of this program, progressions are used. An example is shown on page 60.

60 ◆ The Sport Education Model…and How to Progress to It from Chapter 1

Self-Responsibility/Sportsmanship Report

PRE-SEASON

Team Name: _____ Date: _____

Collectively evaluate the sportsmanship of each of your own team members while playing in today's volleyball game.

Use the following scale:
1 = Rarely (less than 50% of the time)
2 = Sometimes (at least 50% of the time)
3 = Usually (at least 75% of the time)
4 = Always (100% of the time)

Name of player	I encouraged my teammates	I won/lost gracefully	I made correct calls	I was courteous to others

We believe the team displaying the better sportsmanship during our game with _____ was

_____.

Adapted from Schwager and Stylianou, 2012

Days → until end.

Season: Round-robin tournament. Continuing with the use of progressions in the affective domain, the self-assessment turns into above now turns into a potential point scoring mechanism. Along with each student's assessment of their own behavior, the same team question is asked regarding which team had the better sportsmanship during the game. In keeping with progressions, if both teams agree, then that team receives a point contributing to overall scoring.

Self-Responsibility/Sportsmanship Report

Team Name: _____ Date: _____

Rate yourselves on the following scale.

Use the following scale:
1 = Rarely (less than 50% of the time)
2 = Sometimes (at least 50% of the time)
3 = Usually (at least 75% of the time)
4 = Always (100% of the time)

Name of player	I practiced only volleyball skills while practicing	I displayed good sportsmanship to all	I fulfilled my role responsibility in the game	I accepted all calls made by the referee in the game

Adapted from Schwager and Stylianou, 2012

Your team will receive a point if both you and the opposing team in the game agree on which team displayed better sportsmanship.

We believe the team displaying the better sportsmanship during our game with _____ **was** _____ _____.

62 ◆ The Sport Education Model…and How to Progress to It from Chapter 1

All scoring is tallied and shown on the scoresheet. See a sample summary below.

Physical Education Volleyball		
Season Tournament Schedule & Summary		
POINTS		
	Pythonz	Dragons
Day		
1 Pythonz vs Dragons		
score		
2 Pythonz vs Dragons		
score		
3 Pythonz vs Dragons		
score		
4 Pythonz vs Dragons		
score		
5 Pythonz vs Dragons		
score		
6 Pythonz vs Dragons		
score		

Two more aspects of the Sport Education season are noteworthy. Revisiting the *affiliation* aspect mentioned earlier, the model encourages students, once they have their team name and color, to come to physical education class with like colored T-shirts, or perhaps make a banner with the team name.

Another great part is *festivity*. The teacher can create an environment in which the "finals" of a tournament can be played at unusual times, such as lunch or after school, where a larger audience may be able to watch. This is greatly appreciated by students, and creates great school spirit.

Captain's Packet

From James W. Rose

Physical Education

SPORT ___*Volleyball*___
TEAM _____
CAPTAIN _____

Captain's Contract

The captain's responsibilities are:

- ♦ To demonstrate fair play and good sportsmanship at all times.
- ♦ To assist in assigning team player positions.
- ♦ To organize team practices and games.
- ♦ To demonstrate good safety practices.
- ♦ To hand in team roster and team color sheets.
- ♦ To remind the team of the practice and game schedule
- ♦ To review knowledge and skills as needed to prepare for skill challenges, quizzes, and games.
- ♦ To be a "positive leader" showing enthusiasm and to give encouragement at all times.
- ♦ To remind and review class make-up procedures should a teammate miss a practice or game
- ♦ To have each skill checked off by the teacher once the team is "ready."
- ♦ To store this Captain's Packet in the Physical Education office with the teacher unless otherwise agreed upon with the teacher.

I understand and will implement these responsibilities to the best of my ability.

_____

_____

Captains' signatures   Date

Team Roster

Team Name _____

Team Color _____

Captain(s) _____

Equipment Manager(s) _____

Scorekeeper(s) _____

Statistician(s) _____

Sportswriter(s) _____

Official(s) _____

Players:

_____

_____

_____

_____

_____

_____

_____

_____

_____

_____

_____

_____

Player Roles

Captain – First Page

Equipment Manager – To assign, organize, supervise, and ensure that all equipment is treated properly and placed in its correct location following class.

Scorekeeper – To follow and keep track of the scores of all games.

Statistician – To organize, record, and post team and individual statistics.

Sportswriter – To write brief, exciting summaries of games.

Official – To officiate games once "certified." This player must learn rules and "hand signals."

Skill/Knowledge Checklist

The teacher will initial (with date) each skill once it is satisfactorily completed.

Initials	Task
_____	Rules/History
_____	Underhand serve
_____	Forearm pass
_____	Set

Game Preparation Criteria

In order for the teams to compete in games, each must fulfill the following criteria:

- ♦ Completion of the knowledge/skill checklist.
- ♦ Written quiz with a combined team score of 40%.
- ♦ Skill test with a combined team score of 40%.

If a team earns a combined team score greater than 70%, bonus points will be awarded. The amount varies with the team score and each point.

Competition Point System

- ♦ 2 points will be given for each win.
- ♦ 1 point will be given for each tie.
- ♦ 0 points are received for a loss.
- ♦ 1 point may be given for sportsmanship.

   ***** If a team member is absent from class on a quiz/test day, (s)he has 2 class days from their return to school to make-up the missed assessment. Each day beyond this time will cost the team 1 point.

The Sport Education Model...and How to Progress to It from Chapter 1 ◆ 67

***The last, and very important piece, to introduce here is that, in keeping with progressions that are a mainstay of this program in Middle School, intermediate or advanced seasons (units) of a given sport are possible with the Sport Education model. All of the seasons/sports when done for the first time with a class are considered to be *beginning* seasons. Each school's location, size, facilities, etc. become determining factors as to which sports are taught. If a teacher feels that they have exhausted the range of sports to teach, given those factors, then a previously taught sport is taught. **However**, it would be in a more advanced fashion. This implies more advanced skills, strategies, etc., such as a lay-up (basketball), or the overhand serve (volleyball), which were not taught in the beginning season.

Chapter 2 Review

You should now:

- know why movement education and skill themes are beneficial prior to the formal teaching of sport skills.
- know how to determine how much teaching of movement education content (concepts and sub-concepts) and skill-themes may be needed in your teaching situation prior to your formal teaching of sport skills, and how to make a transition into those sport skills (via Sport Education).
- be familiar with "concept transfer."
- know the purpose of Sport Education.
- be able to implement a season of Sport Education, using captains and their packets, student roles, students' sport workbooks, and written and physical tests.

Reading Comprehension Questions

1. How are movement concepts related to sport skills?
2. What is concept transfer, and how can it improve the learning of sport skills?
3. How can the teacher gauge their youngest students' knowledge of movement concepts and sport skills levels? How will this determine to what degree the concepts and skills have been learned?
4. What type of wording should be avoided during these beginning lessons on movement concepts?
5. Name an example of a sport skill that would use the movement education sub-concept of zig-zag.
6. Using Mosston's Spectrum of Teaching Styles, which indirect style (methodology) might be best for the teacher to use when teaching a sport skill using the skill themes approach?
7. How is Sport Education different from traditional models of Physical Education?
8. Rather than being organized by units, what is Sport Education organized by?
9. List four roles that students can choose in Sport Education, in addition to being a player.
10. What is an objective way for an instructor to select a captain for Sport Education?
11. What are some items a student workbook can contain in Sport Education?
12. How would a captain know when his/her team is ready to be observed by the teacher? What tool(s) are at his/her disposal?
13. How are self-responsibility and sportsmanship addressed in this model?
14. What are the phases of a Sport Education season?
15. What types of assessments can occur during Sport Education? Are they subjective or objective?

References

Mosston, M., & Ashworth, S. (1994). *Teaching Physical Education* (4th ed.). New York: Macmillan College Publishing Co.

Siedentop, D. (1994). *Sport Education: Quality PE through Positive Sport Experiences.* Champaign, IL: Human Kinetics.

3

Fitness

Key Concepts:

- There are two types of fitness.
- Health-related fitness is focused on in this program.
- There are four components of health-related fitness.
- Personalizing students' fitness programs relies on fitness testing.
- Grading student fitness is based on percentiles.

Components of Health-Related Fitness

Fitness is so important. There are two kinds of fitness: health-related, and skill-related. Health-related fitness differs from skill-related fitness. In the context of physical education, the former pertains to our health, while the latter could be considered helpful in any wishes we have to be proficient in sport skills. Skill-related fitness includes such components as agility, speed, reaction time, balance, and others. Only health-related fitness will be covered here, primarily due to the fact that it is one of the areas that is assessed in this program.

Health-related Fitness	Skill-related Fitness	
Flexibility	Agility	Power
Muscular Strength	Speed	Coordination
Muscular Endurance	Reaction time	
Cardiovascular Endurance	Balance	

Flexibility refers to the range of motion around a joint. Static stretching of a muscle, or "holding a stretch," is advocated by this author, due to the preponderance of research supporting it. Research has suggested that holding a stretch for 30–45 seconds is effective, such that it allows the muscles (and their Golgi tendon organs) to relax, achieve a further stretch, and subsequently improved flexibility. One of the tests that is frequently used to measure flexibility is the sit-and-reach test.

Muscular strength is the ability of a muscle to contract once. This is often confused with muscular endurance. A common test of muscular strength is the flexed-arm hang, typically given to girls. The student can either jump up to reach a horizontal bar fastened to the wall, or use a chair to stand on to lift one's self to it. The student then stays in a position, with the chin above the bar and the palms facing away from the student, as long as possible. It is a test primarily of the triceps muscle. Sometimes the push-up test is used for measuring muscular strength, although the fact that more than one push-up is being done somewhat misleads the concept.

Muscular endurance is the ability of a muscle to contract repetitively. Examples include push-ups, sit-ups, and others, as long as at **least** two repetitions are performed. Correct form is a must! A test commonly used for muscular endurance is sit-ups.

Cardiovascular endurance is a 4th health-fitness component. It is the heart's ability to contract repeatedly. There are two types or categories of cardiovascular endurance. They are aerobic (with oxygen) and anaerobic (without oxygen). The mile run was commonly used for testing this component. However, more recently, the PACER (Progressive Aerobic Cardiovascular Aerobic Run) Test, a form of the multi-stage fitness test, has been used.

Rationale for Including Fitness in the Program

Naturally, fitness should be included in the overall physical education program. It should have a purpose for students, parents, and the program. Most importantly is the individuality for the students. Your students likely learned about the health-fitness components prior to 5th or 6th grade, but reviewing is always wise. They may have even taken fitness tests, such as the National or Presidential test. If a fitness test was given at the end (or possibly the beginning) of the previous school year, you may have raw data to use. If not, testing students at the beginning of the school year to get data is important for your new students. Why is it important? It is only then that giving the fitness test at the end of the school year (which is done in this program) will show whether improvements are have occurred. This is similar to a pre-test/post-test design. Once again, giving a fitness test to your **new students** at the beginning of the school year is crucial, because you will be giving the test to the all students at year's end.

Most tests will have norms, or percentiles, based on raw scores. Recall that a percentile is not a percentage. The 50th percentile is *average*, with half of the scores of students taking the test nationally falling above the average and half falling below the average. The 99th percentile means that only one percent of students had scores above the raw score corresponding to that (99th) percentile. **Students in this program will be creating their own fitness program to do in class based on these percentiles.** If a student is in the 30th percentile for muscular strength, 50th percentile for cardiovascular endurance, 70th percentile for muscular endurance, and 90th percentile for flexibility, which components is the student more likely to work on, if the goal is to be a well-rounded person, fitness-wise? What are his/her strengths and weaknesses?

The following table shows an example: scores and percentiles for a **12-year old girl**, from the National Fitness Standards, from https://caronefitness.com/mastercourses/acfmastercss/ff1_7_12_css/documents/nationalstandards_girls.pdf

Component	Raw Score	Percentile
Muscular Strength	7 push-ups	30th
Cardiovascular End.	11:05	50th
Muscular Endurance	40 sit-ups	70th
Flexibility	38"	90th

The girl in this case would create her own fitness program, to be done at the beginning of each physical education class. She would focus the most on her muscular strength, which needs the most improvement. She would focus the least on least on her flexibility, which was already at a high level. A wonderful part of this program is that the student is free to do any exercise for her muscular strength (taught and monitored by the teacher) that targets the pectoral muscles, which are the main muscles used in push-ups. The same procedure applies to the other components and exercises. The students are taught what sets and repetitions are, and they create their own program and keep track of their progress.

Integrating Fitness into a Lesson

Use of this information for grading will be explained later in Chapter 5. Although fitness *information* can be reinforced throughout the year, it does not need to be covered in each lesson. It should, though, be the first few lessons of each school year.

For now, let's cover how this fitness program, otherwise known as their class warm-up, is integrated into a lesson. The class can be taught the following procedures. Upon entering the gymnasium or other area, students will take out and set up any mats, etc. for their program. The teacher usually has jump ropes set out for students. Flexibility is to be the first part of the class fitness procedures. Though the body's muscles are more flexible after a light warm-up, due to time constraints and logistics students will stretch gently before anything else. Some students will take longer than others during this part if flexibility was one of their test weaknesses. The effective and efficient aspect of this procedure is that, since the fitness program is individualized, students are on their own time schedule. Some students may be on muscular endurance or muscular strength sooner than others due to this variable.

It is highly recommended to place the cardiovascular endurance part of the warm-up at the end. Since all students **must** use cardiovascular endurance (jump rope/jogging/other) during their warm-up, it is wise to place it at the end of the fitness routine. Those whose cardio is their weakness will likely enter this part earlier, and, therefore, have more (elapsed) time in this phase, but everyone ends the cardio phase at the same time. One prudent reason for ending at the same time is that the teacher can have everyone take...and record... their heart rate simultaneously. Using the concept of progression, the full warm-up routine increases in time throughout the school year. Recall that toward year's end, the fitness test is done again and, typically, gains are seen.

A caveat here: improvement is expected naturally as the body grows. Therefore, the percentiles may vary. In other words, a 12-year-old female student who performs 30 crunches (50th percentile) would need to do 40 as a 13-year-old (still the 50th percentile). As these norms are standardized, note that a 14-year-old would only need to do 30 crunches. As you can see, the norms take growth and maturity into account.

A Sample Gymnasium Set-up for the Fitness Warm-up

C = cones to jog around
 The 3 lines bottom right = jump ropes (enough for the whole class should they so choose)
 The box upper left = mats for e.g. sit-ups
 Small box lower left = folders in which are kept students' individual fitness folders for them to use during class and return at the end of the warm-up.

Gymnasium

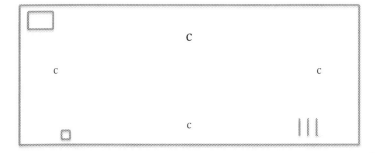

Organization

Keeping students' fitness plans in folders is important. Each time a class enters the gymnasium, a particular class's folder is to be placed on a table or cart. Students then pull their program sheet from the folder and can begin, as they keep it with them throughout the warm-up section of class. Pencils are accessible as well, so that they can record each day's progress. A sample chart for students to use is below. At the end of the warm-up, they return the folder to the cart and the next part of the class can begin.

Component		1	2	3	4	5	6	7	8
DATES:	⇨								
Flexibility	Time stretch held								
Muscular Strength	Exercise Time								
Muscular Endurance	Exercise Sets Reps								
Cardio	Exercise Time Heart Rate Comments								

Use as Part of Grading

Chapter 5 will cover assessment and grading as a whole. It is worth detailing here, though, how the fitness testing scoring will be used. As mentioned, all raw scores are matched to the nearest corresponding percentile. If there is not a clear alignment between the raw score and a percentile, then the lower percentile is used. A comparison is determined from year to year for each component, and grading is based on the *improvement* from the previous year.

Let's say a student was at the 40th percentile for a component on last year's test. This year, the student's score corresponded to the 50th percentile. The increase of 10 percentiles would be counted as a whole grade increase. That is, for this component, the student would receive a full grade increase from what they earned last year. **For this component**, the student would receive a D. Keep in mind that this procedure is used for each component. (Note two exceptions in the next two paragraphs.)

There is an exception to this procedure. Let's say, returning to our earlier example, the 12-year old girl scored in the 90th percentile for flexibility. If she scored at the same percentile the subsequent year (the raw score may change based on age…the child would be a year older), her grade would **not** decrease in the flexibility area because her percentile remained so high…the A range

(90th percentile or above). **Therefore, a student cannot receive lower than their "natural" letter grade anytime they test on a component, if their percentile for that component remains in the higher ranges, such as 70 (C), 80 (B), etc.**

One more caveat must be pointed out. It was mentioned that the 50th percentile is considered average. For any improvement to occur above this level, it physiologically becomes more difficult. Therefore, though a full grade increase takes place for each 10 percentile increase, **once the student's percentile for a score on a test is above the 50th percentile, a full grade increase is given for a percentile rise of only 5%.** A 10% rise above the 50th percentile would then be 2 full grade increases.

The student's **overall fitness grade** for the year is an average of all of the positive and negative percentile changes, expressed in terms of letter grades, from the previous year. For example, let's say the now 13-year old female student above, who received the A for flexibility, received a C, a B, and a B+ for her other component improvements. Her fitness grade would be:

Component	Letter grade	Score used for fitness grade calculation
Flexibility	A	9
Muscular Str.	C	7
Muscular End.	B	8
Cardio Endurance	B+	8.5
		Average = 81.25

The average is 81.25, which would be a B–, which is her fitness grade. This score will be used in Chapter 5 on Assessment.

The student's fitness record can be kept on a document such as the one on page 78.

Sharing with Parents

Parents certainly want to know their child's fitness status. One easy way to share this information is a form such as the one below:

78 ◆ Fitness

Physical Education

Fitness Report

_____   _____
Name   Date

Dear Parent/Guardian,

As you likely know, at Smith Middle School your child participates in Physical Education class. Part of each class is a fitness routine (s)he has created. The exercises your child performs, as well as the time or number of "reps," is based on their fitness test score percentiles from last year. The higher or stronger your child is on a fitness component, the less of it is done in class. Conversely, the area(s) that need improvement are worked on with more intensity.

I'd like to take this opportunity to provide, on the attached paper, the results of your child's most recent fitness test, taken within the last month. You will see the raw score for each component, along with the corresponding national percentile. For informational purposes, the 50th percentile is average, with half the students of your child's grade and gender, nationally, scoring below the raw score, and half scoring above it.

Should you have any questions on this, feel free to contact me at school.

Thank you,

Physical Education teacher

Score/President's Test Percentile/Grade

	5th grade	6th grade	7th grade	8th grade
Flex.				
Musc. Str.				
Musc. End.				
Cardio.				

Chapter 3 Review

You should now:

- know that there are health-related fitness components and skill-related fitness components
- know the four health-related fitness components
- know how to incorporate fitness into your program, personalizing it to students
- know how to use testing results as part of assessment
- know how to share the fitness results with parents

Reading Comprehension Questions

1. What are the four health-related fitness components incorporated into this program?
2. Why should the instructor be testing health-related fitness?
3. When should fitness be tested? Why? What is an option you have for new students who have no record of fitness from a previous school?
4. What is a percentile? What percentile is considered average?
5. Of the four fitness components tested, which one(s) should a student work on the most in class? Why?
6. When should the cardiovascular endurance (aerobic) part of the warm-up be done in this program? Why?

7. How is fitness grading done in this program, for each test? What grade would an improvement of 20 percentiles be (from the previous test) for a given test, if it is above the 50th percentile? Below the 50th percentile?
8. How is a student's overall fitness grade determined?
9. What are two things that can (and should) be done with the fitness test results?

Reference

National Fitness Program, Presidential Fitness Award Program. https://caronefitness.com/mastercourses/acfmastercss/ff1_7_12_css/documents/nationalstandards_girls.pdf

4

Cooperative Activities

Key Concepts:

- ♦ Cooperative activities teaches skills for school and for life
- ♦ Facilitation is the teacher's role
- ♦ Socio-emotional learning (SEL) occurs during cooperative activities

Why Cooperative Activities

"Our country is built upon the concept of teamwork – the kind of teamwork that promotes cooperation and cohesiveness over competition, teamwork in which everyone contributes to a part to make a stronger whole" (Glover & Midura, 1992, p. vii). Cooperation is taught in the youngest grades in schools, in various forms. Socio-emotional learning (SEL) now plays a prominent role in schools. SEL is the process of developing the self-awareness, self-control, and interpersonal skills helpful for school, and ultimately, life. Studies suggest that SEL helps improve academic performance, reduces negative behaviors such as bullying, and helps create a positive classroom climate (Committee for Children, 2023). The physical education environment is particularly suited to cooperative learning, as the three

DOI: 10.4324/9781003423201-5

domains (psychomotor, cognitive, and affective) are utilized, with a significant emphasis on each domain.

The physical challenge involved in cooperative games requires students to interact with each other, so that even the shyest among them become an important part of the group. The affective domain is addressed in that participants have to listen to each other, compliment them for their ideas, and encourage them for their efforts. These skills of listening, praising, and encouraging can be learned at any age. Leaders and followers always come into being when people work together as a team, but everyone is involved in the physical challenges that are cooperative games. It is not the purpose of this book to be a comprehensive resource for cooperative games. This brief review and its implementation of cooperative games within the curriculum during the academic year is the focus of this chapter.

Implementing Cooperative Activities

Facilitation is of utmost importance in the framework of teaching cooperative games. The teacher establishes the atmosphere and the teacher's role is the conduit through which the students, as a class, will solve the problems. Each activity requires the teacher to "set the table" for the students' understanding of what is required of them to be successful. Any equipment is prepared and laid out by the teacher, and (s)he shares the ending, or net result, of each problem. The teacher indicates what "consequences" or penalties are required if a procedure is not followed. (An example is if students are to hold hands for the entire time of the challenge, such as in the game of "Human Knots." If hands are released for any given reason, the group must then start over.) The teacher then allows, actually encourages, students to discuss possible solutions, which addresses both the cognitive and affective domains. This is where thoughtful facilitation is involved. The teacher is careful not to hint at solutions, but rather listens carefully to the dynamic of the class's interaction, and may try to direct attention to positive attempts. The teacher must know ahead of time what solutions will and won't work. Always reminding the class to consider the "next moves" in their sequence becomes paramount.

As with most areas within the physical education program, progressions should be followed when using cooperative games. Chances are that, in middle school, students will come as a class (i.e. a homeroom). However, quite often multiple classes come to physical education class, for various reasons. Reasons can include facilities, scheduling, and other factors. Students in one class may not know students in another class within the same grade. Also, for the youngest grade in the school (typically 5th or 6th), students may not know each other at all, other than those in the same homeroom.

Since it is more than likely than not that students described in the previous paragraph know little about each other, using cooperative games/activities probably would be best introduced during the first part of the scholastic year. This, of course, helps the aforementioned team building. For teachers making use of this book and who are having students work on creating their fitness routine at the beginning of the year, it is a great time to work on the cooperative games. The progressions can be done in numerous ways, such as pair work, followed by small group, large group, and ultimately full class cooperative games. Another progression would be low intensity activity, followed by those that are increasing in intensity, such as Buddy Walkers, and the "tagging" game some people know as Strategy Flag Tag.

A key in timing the progressions of these activities is to sprinkle, or spread, their use throughout the year. From my 30 or so years of experience, using cooperative games can be best achieved at times between the Sport Education seasons. (Again, the term "season" does not refer to an interscholastic sport season.) If you'll recall, one characteristic of the Sport Education model is the length of time spent on a sport. Each of these seasons is of a longer duration than a typical physical education unit. Therefore, devoting a class period to cooperative activities between seasons is prudent. Also, if the sequence of overall activities (not just cooperative activities) is scheduled for optimum fitness building, then the teacher would want the activities to be

84 ◆ Cooperative Activities

of higher intensity progressively through the school year. This assists in students demonstrating their highest fitness at year's end via the fitness test.

A great resource for cooperative games is:

Team Building Through Physical Challenges (Glover & Midura, 1992)

Some suggestions for cooperative games include:

Beginner Challenges

Pairs:
Lead the Blind
Robot
Groups:
The Wall
River Crossing
Stepping Stones
Buddy Walkers
The Whole World in Their Hands challenges

Intermediate Challenges

Groups:
The Jumping Machine
Tarzan of the Jungle
Stepping Stones 2

A sample lesson plan for a class on cooperative games (the first one in a progression) is below. Much of assessing this lesson will be in the affective domain, as cooperative games are probably most associated with this domain. Assessing in the affective domain will be covered in Chapter 5.

Notice the medial summary and review sections of the plan. Though these sections are important in any lesson, students have not experienced these lessons as often as other mainstream lessons. As such, the facilitating is highly important, and debriefing (both medial and final) is important.

Name _____

LESSON PLAN for Cooperative Game _____

Domains _____	Objectives (for this lesson) _____	Date: _____
Physical	To safely lead a sight-deprived classmate around within an area	Grade: 6
Cognitive	To know and abide by the rules	Theme: Cooperative Activities Sub-Theme:
Cognitive		Equipment: warm-up equipment
Affective	To know and abide by the safety rules; show care for partner	Reference

CONTENT	ORGANIZATION AND TRANSITION	TEACHING PROGRESSION AND TEACHING CUES	EVALUATION, MODIFICATION, SUGGESTIONS (per objective)
Warm-up: full warm-up 10 minutes	JRopes, mats laid out, cones	Full warm-up	
Focus: Cooperative Game 15 minutes	Floor spots Into pairs	Remind students of procedures for cooperative activities Today's activity: Lead the Blind Partners chosen by birth month	
	Repeat linear a few times	In pairs, Objective: with your hands on your partner's shoulders, lead your partner across, and then around the room in various ways.	
	Start facing various directions	Switch positions	

(Continued)

CONTENT	ORGANIZATION AND TRANSITION	TEACHING PROGRESSION AND TEACHING CUES	EVALUATION, MODIFICATION, SUGGESTIONS *(per objective)*
Medial Summary 1 minute Continue 5 minutes **Review**: 5 minutes	Formation spread throughout the gym, continuously moving. Floor spots or next to partner	What is your current comfort level? What can you say to your partner to either assure them you are ok, or what you would like instead? Discuss what improvements, from partner, if any, occurred. Give an adjective to describe feelings.	

Chapter 4 Review

You should now:

- know the reasons for including cooperative games and activities in this program.
- know how to introduce and facilitate cooperative activities
- know how to find resources for cooperative games

Reading Comprehension Questions

1. What is socio-emotional learning?
2. Why is the Physical Education environment suited for cooperative games?
3. What is the goal of a cooperative game?
4. What is the role of the teacher in cooperative games?
5. Why is it particularly important to place some cooperative games at the beginning of the school year?
6. Is there only one way to solve cooperative game problems, or are there multiple ways? Justify your answer.

Reference

Glover, D., & Midura, D. (1992). *Team-building through physical challenges.* Champaign, IL: Human Kinetics.

5

Assessment and Grading

Key Concepts:

- ♦ Testing is done in psychomotor, cognitive, and affective domains
- ♦ Each domain has its own weight of grading
- ♦ Students know what they will be tested on
- ♦ An affective grading system is used
- ♦ A Grade Point system is used

How Do We Assess and Grade in Middle School?

The manner in which students are graded in Physical Education class has always been controversial. Rather than discussing the reasons for this, it is more practical to merely explain the system used in this program. We know that assessment falls into two categories....formative assessment and summative assessment. The former is used *during* a unit to monitor student learning and also to provide ongoing feedback that can be used by instructors to improve their teaching. It helps students identify their strengths and weaknesses and target areas that need work. Summative assessment, on the other hand, evaluates student learning at the *end* of the instructional unit by comparing it to a standard or benchmark.

The Domains of Learning

Recall that physical education uses three domains: psychomotor, cognitive, and affective. It is the only school subject to use as its focus the psychomotor domain. Indeed, most people would agree that the psychomotor domain is the crux of physical education class, because much of the subject involves learning movement skills. As such, the psychomotor domain will receive the majority of the weight (50%) when grading. There are numerous places where scores from within this domain will come. Examples include fitness testing results (using this book's philosophy, the *improvement* in yearly fitness testing), and scores on physical skill tests from each Sport Education season. Mind you, there will likely be more than one skill test per season (read: for each sport). Examples might include, for volleyball, the set and the forearm pass. You may remember reading this earlier in the book:

Game Preparation Criteria

In order for the teams to compete in games, each must fulfill the following criteria:

- ◆ Completion of the knowledge/skill checklist.
- ◆ Skill test with a combined team score of 40%.
- ◆ Written quiz with a combined team score of 40%.
- ◆ If a team earns a combined team score greater than 70%, bonus points will be awarded. The amount varies with the team score and each point.

Assigning Percentages of Grading to Each Domain

A 10-point written quiz is given for each sport. You can see from the criteria that each team needs the combined score of 40%. This is to ensure that a sufficient percent of the team understands the rules, etc. That is the cognitive domain, which will count toward 25% of the student's grade.

Likewise, the skill tests are on a 10-point scale, which makes it easier for using percent basis. You will see them alongside the rubrics in the sport booklet. Therefore, students do see the rubrics while they are learning the skill. That is important when knowing one will be tested. Again, the team's aggregate must meet the minimum 40% to enable the team to start the season. Grading in these two domains, the psychomotor and cognitive, are not unusual. They assess what students know and are able to do.

What might be considered different, and progressive, in this program is the grading in the affective domain. Learning in the affective domain has long been viewed as a desired outcome for physical education programs, but usually as a hoped for result, rather than a directly pursued outcome. Affective learning occurs more often when it is planned for and when teaching directly reflects the desired learning outcomes (Hellison, 1995). Some physical education programs have shown positive results in the affective area, Sport Education being one of them (Hastie, de Ojeda, & Luquin, 2011).

A system that I have used assigns point values (both negative and positive) to objectively observed behaviors:

Attendance book code	Meaning	Value
A	Absent	−4 points
L	Late	−2
U	Unprepared	−10
P	lack of physical effort	−1
T	Technical (something physical, such as throwing an object at someone)	−5
W	Homework (not completed)	−5
V	Verbal(ly abusive)	−5
C	Cut class	−15
E	No effort at all	−5
S	Shows great sportspersonship	+2
B	Brings sport workbook to class	+2

It must be noted that each absence counts as a 4-point deduction. However, absences can be made up and the points retrieved. Possible times to make up absences include at lunch, after school, or another agreed upon time. A make-up would be considered the full class activities, which likely include the warm-up, the skill practice or game situation. The latter is at the discretion of the teacher.

These behaviors are from teacher observation. They are recorded during each class on the class roster or other daily marking tool. At the end of each marking period, scores from all three domains are used, with weights, in calculating the grade. In converting numerical and letter grades, the following scale is used, and is representative of a developmental point scale:

Grade Point Explanation (From J. Rose)

A+	9.5 +
A	9.0–9.49
A–	8.8 – 8.99
B+	8.5–8.79
B	8.0–8.49
B–	7.8 – 7.99
C+	7.5–7.99
C	7.0–7.49
C–	6.8–6.99
D+	6.5–6.79
D	6.0–6.49
D-	5.8–5.99
Inc.	below 5.8

A sample grade sheet from a whole school year is below (p. 92). Notice that the Cognitive (25%) and Affective (25%) domains average together (C/A), and that the C/A and the Psychomotor domain (50%) average together yielding the student's final grade for the year. Again, the Psychomotor domain contains an average of the skill tests and the fitness test improvement (or decreased) score.

Name	Cognitive 25%				Affective 25%				C/A avg.	Psychomotor 50%					Grade
	tests			Avg	AGS	absences	Avg.			tests			Fitness	Avg.	
	1	2	3							1	2	3			
Lena	A	B	B	8.3	−5	1	9.1	8.725		F	F	D		2.66	5.68
	9	8	8							2	0	6			I
	A+	B	F	7.5	−1	1	9.5	8.5		A+	A+	A+			
Ben	9.5	8	5							10	10	10		10	9.25
															A
Sara	D	F	D	4.7	−23	1	7.3	5.65		F	F	F		2	3.82
	6	0	6							0	4	2			I
Alex	C	A	B	8.5		0	10	9.25		A+	A+	F		8.59	8.92
	7.5	9.5	8.5							10	10	5.79			B+

(AGS represents the Affective Grading System score.)

Assessment and Grading ◆ 93

An explanation of Alex's scores and grade follows.
Step 1: The Cognitive domain:

- On the first of the three written tests throughout the year he received a 7 of 10 for a C. For grading purposes, from the Grade Point Explanation it is a 7.49 (the highest within the ange). This rounds to 7.5.
- On the second of the three written tests throughout the year he received 10 out of 10 for an A. For grading purposes, from the Grade Point Explanation it is a 9.49 (the highest within the range). This rounds to 9.5.
- On the third of the three written tests throughout the year he received a 8 of 10 for a B. For grading purposes, from the Grade Point Explanation it is a 8.49 (the highest within the range). This rounds to 8.5.

The average of 7.5, 9.5, and 8.5 is 8.5, his Cognitive average.
Step 2: Within the Affective domain, Alex had no deductions and was never absent. His grade in this domain is a 10.
The average of his Cognitive and Affective areas is 9.25.
Step 3: The Psychomotor domain:

- On the first of the two physical tests throughout the year he received a 10 of 10 for a A+. For grading purposes, from the Grade Point Explanation it remains 10 (the highest within the range).
- On the second of the two physical tests throughout the year he received a 10 of 10 for a A+. For grading purposes, from the Grade Point Explanation it remains 10 (the highest within the range).
- On the fitness test, Alex performed poorly, compared to last year's percentiles, and received a 3, which is an F. For grading purposes, from the Grade Point Explanation, we give the benefit of the doubt and it is the highest of the INC range at 5.79.

The average of his Psychomotor scores of 10, 10, and 5.79 is 8.59.

Step 4: The average of his C/A and psychomotor is 8.92. His final grade is B−.

This procedure can also be followed for quarterly grades, mid-year grades, etc. For these the fitness test score would not be included as they have not occurred yet.

Chapter 5 Review

You should now:

- know how the assessment system advocated here differs from traditional methods.
- know how to assess in each of the three domains.
- know how to use percentiles for grading (any improvement on) the fitness test.
- know how to report fitness test scoring to parents.

Reading Comprehension Questions

1. In this program, which domain receives the greatest weight when grading? Why?
2. From a previous chapter's discussion, for what score/ grade will the teacher need the previous year's scores?
3. How are sport skills tested in this program? Which domain would they count for?
4. What are two behaviors in the Affective Grading System that are a minimum 10 points off of a student's daily grade?
5. Can the points for either of these actions be retrieved? If so, how?
   Which two domains' scores are averaged together to average with the physical domain's score to yield a student's final grade?

References

Hastie, P. A., de Ojeda, D. M., & Luquin, A. C. (2011). A review of research on Sport Education. *Physical Education & Sport Pedagogy, 16*(2).

Hellison, D. (1995). *Teaching responsibility through physical activity.* Champaign, IL: Human Kinetics

6

Intramurals

Key Concepts:

- ◆ Intramurals is an extension of the physical education program
- ◆ A "blind draft" is essential for having fair, unbiased teams
- ◆ Contests follow a round-robin format with each team likely playing the same team more than once
- ◆ The scoring system includes more than just points for a win

Intramurals literally means "competing within the student body" (Merriam-Webster). When you were in middle school, did you school have intramurals? Sometimes intramurals can be class vs. class within a grade. Other times, Physical Education conducts intramurals. Intramurals can be considered an extension of the Physical Education program, and a lead-up to interscholastic sports, the latter of which is not the topic of this book.

Your school's (district's) physical education philosophy is likely to dictate the form that intramurals will take. Relative to the philosophy of this book, intramurals is a progression from physical education. It is voluntary for students, and perhaps those who are more athletic, and have time, will want to participate. However, if you are following this book's program principles, it is likely that a substantial number of students may participate because they feel comfortable with what they are learning in physical education class via the Sport Education model.

DOI: 10.4324/9781003423201-7

Team Selection

In this program, you'll want fairness regarding how teams are selected. It is logical for the teacher to choose a captain for each team; however it most prudent to do so based on objective criteria. One such criterion might be the student's physical education grade which you learned about in Chapter 5. A student with a good physical education grade is likely to have more knowledge of sports, effective communication, and be highly motivated. After a captain, teams are chosen using a *blind draft.*

If you are not familiar with a blind draft, players are selected by a captain based on a self-rating system. However, the captain does not know whom they are selecting. To clarify, a two-sided sheet (see below) is provided to all intramural participants. On one side they place their name. The other side will have the intramural sports to be contested during the school year. Each student rates his/her knowledge or experience for each sport. The captain then sees the self-rated part of the sheets, and selects the individuals the captain wants. Since the individuals are on the same team for the whole year, the captain looks for a well-rounded group of students. That is, the captain would not want to select only those who have experience in football. Rather, the captain wants some students who have some experience with football (but perhaps not volleyball) and some who experienced in volleyball (but perhaps not soccer), etc. Teams are then posted for all to see. A sample sheet also follows.

Intramurals Blind Draft page 1

_____

Your name

Intramurals Blind Draft page 2
Rate yourself for each of the following sports

Soccer		Football	
_____	Highly experienced	_____	Highly experienced
_____	Somewhat experienced	_____	Somewhat experienced
_____	No experience	_____	No experience

Volleyball		Floor hockey	
_____	Highly experienced	_____	Highly experienced
_____	Somewhat experienced	_____	Somewhat experienced
_____	No experience	_____	No experience

Softball		Cross-country running	
_____	Highly experienced	_____	Highly experienced
_____	Somewhat experienced	_____	Somewhat experienced
_____	No experience	_____	No experience

Basketball	
_____	Highly experienced
_____	Somewhat experienced
_____	No experience

Sample Intramural Teams

TEAM 1	TEAM 2	TEAM 3
The Riders	*The Jokers*	*The Eagles*
Capt: Joseph C	Captain: Marissa H	Captain: Erika S
Aaron G	Anthony R	Maria J
Gabriella R	Anastasia B	Carlos Q
Tina G	Sal T	Ted O
Anthony B	Victor T	Juan S

Scheduling of Intramurals

Rarely have I come across a middle school with only one physical education teacher in it. This can be important because of the officiating that must be done for each game. Teachers often receive a stipend for organizing and officiating intramurals, and intramurals is one of the many activities that are built into the teacher's contract. As intramurals occurs typically after school, having more ability to create a rotating schedule of teachers as officials is beneficial.

A round robin of games is created with each team playing the same number of games. Often teams will play the same team multiple times. The captain, after each contest, would circle the winning team and place the score next to it. A schedule may look something like this:

Intramurals Schedule

VOLLEYBALL

Official	Date	Teams
A.T.	11/19	Riders vs. Jokers 9-7
C.G.	11/23	Jokers vs. Eagles
A.T.	11/29	Riders vs. Eagles
C.G.	12/2	Riders vs. Jokers
A.T.	12/3	Jokers vs. Eagles
C.G.	12/8	Riders vs. Eagles
A.T.	12/9	Championship

Scoring of Intramurals

Scoring is progressive within this program's philosophy. Intramurals is often a lead-up to interscholastic sports (not included in this book). Therefore:

For a win = 2 points per contest
For a tie = 1 point per team

In addition, statistics are maintained for each team BY the team. A sample scoring sheet is contained in this chapter on page 106; this one is for football. A sample statistics sheet is page 107.

Intramural Sports Rules

As this is a developmental endeavor, a step away from the interscholastic athletics, some students may not know the rules of each sport. Therefore, it is wise to provide Rules Sheets for each sport to the captain. A couple of samples are below, in boxes:

Intramural Cross-Country Rules

1. Need a minimum of 5 people to participate.
2. Each person is assigned a number at the end of each race, which is their actual order of finish of all people in that race. This number will be on a 3×5 card. The team with the lowest added up sum of their own **first five** finishers receives 5 points. The team with the second lowest score receives 3 points. (6th and 7th place finishers from each team are tie-breakers.)
3. Each athlete that finishes within the special designated time for each course, but does not finish in the top 5, receives an extra point. (Only valid on official teams…teams with the minimum number of athletes to score.)

Cross-Country Intramural Procedure

- walk the course, stretch
- put on pinnies
- race
- receive finish cards in "chute" (finish area)
- put team name and your name on it
- Captain must collect cards from team WITH the information on it
- go to central area while scoring is done

Intramural Lacrosse Rules

1. Halves are 35–40 minutes long
2. Goggles must be worn at all times
3. Need 8 people:

   At the beginning of the game, must have 1 goalie, 2 in the defensive area, 3 in the middle area, and 2 in the offensive area.

   During play, each team must have a minimum of 4 people in the defensive end (including the goalie) at all times, and 3 in the offensive end at all times. Penalty for infraction, see below.
4. Start with a face-off of 2 middies, cradles back to back.
5. No offensive players are permitted in the crease, which goes around the goal. This includes players' sticks. Penalty – possession given to the defending team at mid-line.
6. The only contact permitted in the game is cradle to cradle.

   Penalty – if the team whose player commits the foul is on offense, possession goes to the defensive team. If the team whose player commits the foul is on defense, the violator goes to the penalty box for 1 minute. FOUR FOULS BY AN INDIVIDUAL WILL MEAN EJECTION.

---keep in mind, if a player goes to the penalty box, a team must still have 4 in the defensive end and 3 in the offensive end.

7. If a ball gets trapped under something, the team whose player did not touch it last receives possession. However, if a shot was taken and it goes out of bounds, the closest player to the ball when it went out gets possession (or their team).

Sample Intramural Scoring

Team	Soccer	Running Total	Football	Running Total	Volleyball*	Running Total	Hockey	Total
Riders	2 1	3	2 2 2	9	10 8 10 9 9 3	58	2 2 2	64
Jokers	2 1 2	5	2 2 2 2	13	8 8 8 11	48	2 1 2	53
Eagles	2 2 2	6	2 2 2	12	8 8 8 8 5	49	2 1 2 2 2	58

*Notice that for Volleyball there is rally scoring, rather than a normal 21-point game.

Intramural Football (Sample Statistics Sheet)

Name	TD (run and caught)	TD passes	Extra Points	Field Goals	Interceptions
Aaron	I I I I				
Anthony	I I	I	II		II
Maria	III				
Gabriella	III	I			I
Anastasia	II				
Carlos					
Tina	II				
Sal		I			I
Ted		II			II
Anthony	IIIII				
Victor	III				
Juan	II				
Joseph		II			
Marissa			I		

Each I denotes a tally.

Chapter 6 Review

You should now:

- know how to set up unbiased teams through a blind draft.
- know how to create schedules and statistics for intramurals.

Reading Comprehension Questions

1. How are teams selected for intramurals?
2. What is a blind draft?
3. What is a captain's responsibility in a blind draft?
4. What is a player's responsibility in a blind draft?

7

Summary and Student Success Stories

*Disclaimer: all names have been changed in order to protect student privacy and confidentiality.

This book has presented progressive methodology to teach middle school physical education. Depending on your experience level, you may have been familiar with parts of it. Have you asked yourself what you want your students to graduate with regarding their physical education skill set as they move toward high school?

Properly teaching Movement Education and Skill Themes is still only taught, in my estimation, by significantly less than 50% of teachers at the elementary level. Therefore, the learning of concepts and sport skills by students entering your program likely needs to be strengthened. By your delving into and gaining a rich understanding of teaching using those models, you can make your students', and your own, experience all the better as they transition to your middle school program.

Those middle school students who are not the highest skilled are often the most pleasantly surprised in the Sport Education season. Each has his/her own overall strengths. Often a diligent student does well on a sport's written quiz and skill test. It is not uncommon for this student to be selected by the teacher as a captain for the next sport, regardless of the student's gregariousness

DOI: 10.4324/9781003423201-8

or knowledge of that next sport. In this situation, the student, with teacher guidance, learns how to work as a leader for the team and typically does quite well. You will find that the teammates help out. Why is this? This is because the team uses the *affiliation* aspect of the model to work together and be part of something. Certainly they want to win, but more importantly, they have fun helping each other.

There are several accounts of students who had various types of special positive experiences from participating in this program. Each one should provide you with reinforcement of the program's value and validity. Just as a tremendous amount of work and planning goes into any successful venture, fully understanding this program and taking the time to do it right is rewarding for everyone. My career satisfaction using this program remains high, which of course is why I share it with you. The students' satisfaction, while not understanding it while they are in the midst of it, was evident and a few success stories follow.

One story that comes to mind is a 4th grader who happened to be very good at basketball. In class we were working on the basketball dribble (using the Skill Themes approach) and they were challenged to dribble bilaterally under control to discover what concepts were being used. This boy, adept at dribbling, was, let's just say, bored. I approached him before he went off-task. I then asked him to find other ways to dribble bilaterally (intra-task variation). Not understanding what I meant, I asked him to dribble between his legs. This was not easy for him. This task met the criteria and objective of the lesson, and he learned something (and actually enjoyed it).

Pam was a slight-framed 6th grader. Her cardio was not very strong, which she discovered on her fitness test. Based on the percentiles, she created her own program that included a lot of jogging at the end. She would jog as long as 10 minutes…for her quite good. I started jogging with her one day in class (I was also the Cross-Country coach) and was complimenting her on her newfound ability. What I was really trying to do was open her thoughts to the possibility of running Cross-Country. I was not successful. Rather, she felt good enough about herself to join the

Summary and Student Success Stories ◆ 111

Volleyball team at school. Her fitness transformation translated into an increase in confidence and joining a sport.

Erika was new to our school as a 6th grader. She was a very athletic girl. As a new student, we had no fitness data on her from her former school. Since all of the students in her class were working on creating their fitness program at the beginning of the school year, based on their scores from the previous year, Erika needed to take the fitness tests. This was actually very motivating for her. Not only did she then get to join her classmates in creating and implementing her program (enjoying it as well), but the test also served as a "lab" because of the fitness knowledge that was taught the first part of each school year.

Alejandro was quiet 5th grader. He was a very good student, but not the best when it came to sports skills. During his 5th grade year, he enjoyed learning sport skills in physical education class and was becoming competent with them. He did have a good understanding of movement concepts from being in the younger grades, but his body had not yet caught up to his cognitive ability. He joined intramurals that year and gained experience as we had a combined 5th and 6th grade intramural program, and the captains were 6th graders. When he got to 6th grade, he was selected (by the teacher) as a captain. During the year, his experience in Physical Education class helped him immensely. Keep in mind that we were using Sport Education in class, so he had the benefit of learning movement concepts and skill themes in the elementary school program, and Sport Education and intramurals in Middle School. Suffice to say that he successfully joined the basketball and baseball teams in the Middle School.

Dan was very bright and athletic. In 5th grade he was a natural with his sport skills, and he had internalized the movement concepts well. In both 5th and 6th grades he participated in Intramurals, and was successful as both a player and a captain. I particularly recall his participation in our Cooperative Games, where he offered suggestions for solving problems, and encouraged others as if he were a teacher himself. I also vividly recall an interscholastic Cross-Country race he was in as an 8th grader. As his coach, I had confidence in him, but one situation stands out. He was in second place with about 200 yards to finish. He looked at me as he ran by me and said, "I got this guy." Of course I was happy to hear that, but I didn't know who else had heard it. He did win, but we had a nice talk after the race about how else he could have handled that situation and kept his emotions in check. He understood. Fast forward to 3 years later as a high school junior, no longer at our school. He still ran Cross-Country, this time as a Varsity athlete. As a fan, I tended to watch these races, and this was the County Championship. His team won an award, and all of the athletes received medals. Do you know what he did with his? He walked up to me, handed me his medal, and said, "This is for you. Thanks." Wow... enough said, right? His "affective domain" had certainly grown and remained strong!

Twins Nathalie and Nancy were new to the school in 7th grade. They were not experienced in sports skill/athletics at all. They were too old for our intramural program, but of course could participate in the interscholastic program. They did not. However, I believe, due to our physical education program of Sport Education, the girls quickly became comfortable with physical education. They learned the sport skills in a setting conducive to making friends. Sure enough, for the winter season they both joined the basketball team, and for the spring season, one played soccer and the other played softball. It was rewarding to see how two girls who entered the school so shy could end up in a short four months fully integrated into our physical education program.

These are just a few of the many examples. Each one brought its own rewarding satisfaction for the student and for myself. It is my hope that you achieve similar results with your implementation of this program.

Index

affective learning 90
affiliation 37, 62, 110
Ashworth, S. 35
assessment: formative 88; peer 54; self 60; summative 88; types 88; workbook 37
authentic sport experiences 3
authenticity 36

blind draft 97–99
body awareness 6–10, 17, 21, 34

Captain's Packet 52–53, 63
cardiovascular endurance 71, 72, 74
class warm-up 73
cognitive domain 90, 93
concept transfer theory 33–34
cooperation 81
cooperative activities 81–82; beginner challenges 84; implementing 82–84; intermediate challenges 84; lesson plan 84–86; progressions 83; resource 84; seasons 83
cooperative games 82, 111; *see also* cooperative activities
Cross-Country coach 110

domains of learning 89

festivity 62
fitness 17; cardiovascular endurance 71; flexibility 71; grading 76–77, 79; gymnasium 75; health *vs.* skill-related 71; integrating in lesson 73–74; kinds 70; muscular endurance 71; muscular strength 71; norms/percentiles 72; organization 75–76; program 72–73; sharing with parents 77–78; warm-up 75

flexibility 71, 73, 76, 77
formative assessment 88

game: preparation 66, 89; tagging 33
Gosset, M. 35
grading 76–77, 89–94
guided discovery methodology 35
gymnasium 17, 33, 75

health-related fitness 70; *vs.* skill-related fitness 71
higher other thinking skills (HOTS) 2
Human Knots 82

instant activity 17
interscholastic sports 36, 83, 93, 103
intramurals: cross-country procedure 104; cross-country rules 103; definition 96; football 107; Lacrosse rules 104–105; rules 103; sample scoring 106; sample team 100; schedule 101–102; scoring 103; team selection 97–99

learning: affective 90; domains of 89; socio-emotional 37, 81
lesson plans: cooperative activities 84–86; movement education 17–21; skill-themes 22–28
line-to-line (LTL) 17, 18, 19

Manipulation of Objects 9, 10–13, 15, 22
minutes sheets: movement education 9–10; skill-themes 13–16
Mosston, M. 35
movement education: lesson plans 17–21; minutes sheets 9–10; teaching the concepts 8–10; themes of awareness 6–8

114 ◆ Index

multi-activity approach 2, 6
muscular endurance 71–74, 76
muscular strength 71–74, 76

new students 72, 111
non-consecutive fashion 8

parents 3, 72, 77
peer assessment 54
physical education: cognitively
  2; domains 89; emotionally 2;
  percentages of grading 89–93;
  physically 2
pre-test/post-test design 72
preseason 37
problem-solving 4, 6, 35
progressions 8, 59, 60, 67, 83
Progressive Aerobic Cardiovascular
  Aerobic Run (PACER) 71
psychomotor domain 89

safety 24, 64
Schmidt, R. A. 11, 33
seasons 36, 67, 83
self-manipulation 22
Siedentop, D. 3, 36
skill-related fitness 70; health-related
  fitness *vs.* 71
skill-themes approach 2, 10–12;
  lesson plans 22–28; minutes sheets
  13–16
socio-emotional learning (SEL) 37, 81

Spectrum of Teaching Styles 35
Sport Education 32; Captain's Packet
  52–53, 63; captain's responsibilities
  64; competition point system
  66–67; concept transfer chart
  33–34; game preparation criteria
  66; implementation 36–37; peer
  assessment 54–55; player roles 65;
  preseason 37; purpose 36; roles
  36–37; season organization 59;
  self-responsibility/sportsmanship
  report 60–61; skill/knowledge
  checklist 66; team captains 52–53;
  team roster 65; teams 52–53;
  volleyball *see* volleyball
summative assessment 88

tagging game 33
teacher's role 82
team roles 59
transition 18–21, 23–26, 32–33, 109

volleyball: basic rules 39–40; forearm
  pass 44–45; history 39; positioning
  41; rotation 42; scoring 62; season
  55–58; setting 46–47; spike and
  the serve 48; testing skills 49–50;
  workbook 51–52

wording 32
workbook 37, 38, 52; assessment 37;
  volleyball 51–52

Printed in the United States
by Baker & Taylor Publisher Services